GET STINKING
RICH
SOLVING OTHERS'
PROBLEMS

Big Problems. Big Solutions.
Big Money.

VAIDYA SELVAN

are not intended to imply that similar outcomes will be achieved by others.

Business Risk Acknowledgment: By using the information in this publication, you acknowledge that starting and operating a business involves inherent risks, including but not limited to market volatility, competition, operational challenges, and the possibility of financial loss. The strategies presented may not be suitable for every individual or situation.

Limitation of Liability: The author and publisher disclaim any liability for direct, indirect, incidental, consequential, or special damages arising from the use or misuse of the information contained in this publication. No liability is accepted for loss of profits or other commercial damages.

Due Diligence: You are encouraged to conduct independent research, perform due diligence, and seek professional guidance before implementing any strategies or making decisions based on the content of this publication.

Market Conditions Disclaimer: Business environments, market dynamics, and regulatory frameworks change frequently. Strategies that are effective at one time may not be applicable at another. Always adapt your approach to current conditions and seek up-to-date information.

Personal Responsibility: Your success or failure is ultimately your responsibility. This publication provides general information and strategies, but your results will depend on your implementation, effort, and decision-making.

Educational Use Only: This publication is intended for informational and educational use only. It presents general principles that may have been successful in various contexts but may not be appropriate for your specific circumstances.

Acknowledgment of Risk: By reading and using this publication, you acknowledge that you have read, understood, and accepted this disclaimer. You agree to assume all risks associated with the use of any strategies or advice contained herein.

Acknowledgments

I extend my heartfelt gratitude to my beloved family-Sasidevi, Shruthi, and Shrish for their unwavering support, inspiration, and encouragement throughout the creation of this book. Your belief in me has been the driving force behind this endeavor.

There comes a time in life when we realize that we are merely passing through, our time is finite, and everything we accumulate is temporary. In that moment of clarity, we understand the importance of simplifying our lives, focusing on what truly matters, and letting go of the excess that distracts us from our true purpose. We've been conditioned to chase money endlessly, often forgetting to live our lives truly. But each of us has the power, responsibility, and obligation to leave behind something useful and meaningful to others.

This book is my humble attempt to do just that: to leave a lasting footprint that may serve and empower future generations.

I am also deeply grateful to those who brought their talents to this project: my editor and proofreader, Jamie, for sharpening the message; Farah, my graphic designer, for visually shaping the book's identity; and Milos, my cover designer, for creating a striking first impression. Your contributions were invaluable in bringing this vision to life. I thank you.

Table of Contents

Introduction

What motivates us? Most people will say pain, but it may also be pleasure. And they're right up to a point. But there's something even deeper. Something that pushes us further, makes us stay up late, get back up after our failures, and keeps us going even when there's no applause or a pat on our backs.

Its purpose.

Purpose gives our actions meaning. It fuels our sense of pride and fulfillment. And when that purpose helps other people? That's when everything shifts. That's when we grow. That's when we win.

Here's what I've learned:

When someone else is counting on you to show up, you are on time and are punctual. You also get the job done as promised.

But on the flipside, when it comes to you, and it's you versus your excuses, fears, or doubts, it becomes a tough road for you to execute on your promises to yourself, and you don't partake in doing it. You refuse to listen to your inner voice, fail to act on it, and get the job done. Why is it that you are pushing yourself to the back seat and everyone else to the front? Are you willing to work for someone and make them rich, Versus working for yourself and making yourself rich?

So I'll ask you what someone once asked me:

What's your purpose in life?

What do you have that can help someone else? Why do you get up in the morning? What do you look forward to doing each day? What's your true purpose? Without purpose, our lives would be, to put it simply, a meaningless existence.

I've come to realize that I'm most effective at helping people by providing inspiration, motivation, and authentic, time-tested real-world information, especially when it comes to finances, business, and building a fulfilling life. I know a thing or two about money, business, and life. I have breathed it, lived it, and experienced it. And my battle scars are here to prove it. Just like you, we all have had our share of the good, bad, mean, and the worst. That is what life is all about. A mix of the best and the worst that a man or a woman has to offer. This is what it takes to be Human today. And when you look back at history, nothing has changed. That essence of Human life and behavior remains.

But did I always know all about life? Not really and sort of. Did I know everything? No. No one does? It is impossible to know everything. An open mind is an open book waiting to imbibe knowledge through its inner curiosity to learn, apply, and thrive. *No one can feed a closed mind.* It is closed from within, and no one from the outside can open it. When this happens, the mind gets narrower, defensive in its own beliefs, and resists any change to its belief system.

Why? Because it is afraid.

Afraid of being judged.

Afraid of standing and speaking up.

Afraid of what people might think. Will they think that I do not know enough or that I am not good enough for them?

But everything changed when I stopped focusing inward on **myself** and started learning more about **them and what they wanted**. I was seeking inner validation from my inner self through introspection, but at the same time, I was looking outward for ways to serve others.

I stopped asking, *"Will they like me?"* and started asking, *"How can I help them succeed?"* Here we are redirecting the same energy to flow through a different pathway.

That shift from ego to service is where money lives. It's where our purpose resides, and it is where our power originates. Find their pain point and help solve it.

I started small with eight people on my couch. I offered to buy them lunch so they would show up.

And they did, and they listened.

Not because I had all the answers, but because I had something they needed. Something that helped them. They wanted real solutions to their life problems. Once I opened up and let them know what I had to offer, they told others, and that small group started getting larger and larger. Soon, it was a full house.

And just like that, it started progressing into larger and larger groups.

No, I wasn't building apps. I wasn't inventing tech. I wasn't selling magic pills, snake oil, trendy beauty creams, or promising them the moon.

I was solving their real-life problems in a way that made people feel seen, heard, understood, and empowered.

And here's what I want you to understand right from the start:

Why does Solving Others' Problems Pay Much More than working "Hard" at a job?

Here's the difference. You can work 18-hour days, sweat through your shirt, and still stay broke. But solve one valuable problem for someone, and now you're in business. Solve it for ten people? You're scaling. Solve it for a thousand? You're rich. Keep it moving and scaling. Ultimately, you will fall into the category of Billionaires.

"Working hard is noble. But solving problems is profitable."

Why is the World able, ready, and willing to Pay Problem Solvers?

People are overwhelmed. Frustrated. Tired of struggling. The moment you make something easier, faster, better, cheaper, or clearer for them, they pay attention. And if it truly helps them, they are prepared to pay you for it by opening their wallets.

Not out of guilt. But out of gratitude.

Know What the World Needs - And What It's Waiting For

The world doesn't want more stuff. It wants relief for people's problems.

It is waiting for solutions.

And it's waiting for people who pay attention and act on it to solve them. People who ask, *What's not working? What's hurting? What's missing? What solution can I bring to the table to help solve? These are the people who may have the potential to make it to the top 1%.*

The vast majority will be followers, just blindly following the masses without ever asking questions. Where the herd goes, they go blindly, clueless, directionless, and with no purpose. They may also be heading in the wrong direction or, worse, towards predators.

What's your preference? Do you want to be a follower or a producer? Not that being a follower is bad, but being a producer can bring about change in this world and make you wealthy beyond your wildest dreams.

Do You Have What It Takes to Solve Others' Problems?

The better question might be: **To start, how can I help just one person first?**

19

And that's where it starts, not with a viral launch or a fancy brand.

It starts with that first infant step by helping one person improve their life. One burden lifted.

Even if one person says, *"Wow, thank you for helping me solve this problem. I have been waiting too long to find a solution."*

That will be a game-changer for you, and it will be the boost you need to move and help many more people.

If you can do that over and over, you've got something priceless and something brewing inside you.

The New Gold Rush: Pain Points, Not Products

Forget chasing trends or copying what everyone else is doing. The real gold isn't in the product—it's in the **problem**.

Find the pain, meet the need, and fix the frustration. It's that simple when taken down to the nitty-gritty.

That's your goldmine.

Where Do Big Problems Hide?

They hide in plain sight. In everyday life.

In systems that are broken. In clunky experiences.

In confusion. In stress. In wasted time and in places where unnecessary struggle exists.

Where people say, *"This shouldn't be this hard"* or *"Why do we have it set up this way?"*—that's where you should be looking.

The "Problem Solver" Mindset

You're not just chasing success. You're building usefulness.

Start thinking like a doctor who sees symptoms no one else notices. Or a mechanic who hears sounds that others miss. You're not here to sell. You're here to serve.

That mindset separates noise from value. By doing so, you will stand out from the crowd and create a brand for yourself.

Stop Chasing Money. Be Real. Be Genuine. Be Authentic, and the World will follow you.

The World is looking for people who say who they are and are willing to stay timeless, no matter the noise outside.

People don't trust hype. They trust real and Authentic.

When you stop trying to impress and start trying to help, everything changes. You'll attract not just clients, but fans and ambassadors to your brand. These are People who believe in what you do, because what you do *actually helps them.* This is how social proof crosses over to trust and loyalty.

The Invisible Power of Curiosity and Empathy

Want to solve more problems?

Start listening better.

Ask better questions. Step into other people's shoes. Feel what they feel. Curiosity shows you where their problems are. Look and you will see them staring at you. Most people will miss them. Empathy will show you how to fix them.

Turn Frustration into Fortune

People's biggest frustrations are your biggest opportunities.

Every complaint is a clue. Every "Why is this so hard?" is just a breadcrumb in a much larger pile of breadcrumbs.

Follow the trail. Find the pain. Fix it and get paid. You may even be able to charge a premium for it because people will be willing to pay you top dollars. That's the simple formula. It seems very simple. But how many of you will do it?

So here's the truth:

If you want to get **stinking rich**, stop chasing money—and start chasing **problems**.

Help one person, then another. Eventually, the whole World will have its wallets open to seek your expertise.

Build a system around the solution to that problem, then move on to solve many more problems. Soon, you will have your hands full and not know what to do with the money coming in.

It's not about the money, but it's also about the money.

It's also about the principle of bringing about a solution to a problem that has been in existence for years, sitting in plain sight, and no one has done anything to bring about a solution to that problem.

Once you have the solutions for various problems at hand, do not stay put or get comfortable. Keep moving.

Duplicate it. Multiply your impact. Your income will follow, and your efforts and answers will be unstoppable for generations. This is how generational wealth gets created. As history bears witness, no one has ever gotten rich by trading time for money or by chasing a paycheck.

Unstoppable Wealth. That's what this book is about.

Not fluff. Not theory.

However, the real path to creating wealth is to make someone else's life better and more comfortable. Giving them what they want by providing solutions to their problems.

PART 1

FINDING BIG PROBLEMS

THE IMPOSSIBLE CATCH-UP

CHAPTER 1

The Science of Pain: What Makes a Problem "Big"?

Let's be honest: life is full of problems, mostly man-made. From the moment you wake up groggy, annoyed by your alarm, to the moment you fall into bed, you're navigating a series of mini-struggles. Your phone battery dies. Traffic is a mess. A package arrives late, and your coffee's cold. A coworker sends another confusing email.

These aren't life-shattering. They're just noise. But occasionally, we hit something bigger. Something that disrupts us. Something that makes us pause, ache, worry, and be stressed.

That's pain.

Not just physical pain, but emotional, financial, relational, and even spiritual pain.

That's the kind of problem this book is talking about.

Real wealth is created when you can step into someone else's shoes and chaos and bring them clarity, peace, and answers by giving them a solution to their problem at hand.

Let me give you a quick example:

Imagine a person standing on the banks of a river. He looks at the river, complains that the water is a little muddy, and wishes it were clearer. On the other hand, downstream from him, another person is drowning in the current, has his arms high up, and is screaming for help.

Now, which one of them will be willing to pay anything for an immediate solution? The guy drowning has a problem and is seeking help immediately. He is in a life-threatening situation. He may even be ready to sign the deeds to all his properties to you to save his life. A muddy river may not be an immediate problem for a guy standing on the embankment and watching the river flow by, since he has no immediate problem that needs to be solved right away. And he will, for sure, not be willing to pay to clean up the muddy river.

People will pay when they're drowning.

When they're desperate, when they're stuck, when they are lost, when their problem has become too heavy to carry alone, that's why understanding real pain is your secret weapon.

Before you create a business, write a book, build an app, offer a service, or launch a brand, you've got to learn this skill: the ability to identify the kinds of problems that make people pay attention. The ones that hit deep, affect daily life, and carry emotional or financial weight. These are the hallmarks you should be looking for. You are not doing it just for the money, but to make a much wider imprint in this World by providing solutions to others' problems. It also does not mean you should exploit others or take advantage of the adverse conditions they are in or when they are in an emergency.

Because here's the truth:

You don't need to solve *every* problem to be successful.

You just need to solve **one big one**. Really, well. And be the best at it.

But not all problems are created equal. And if you waste your energy chasing the small ones, the "mild annoyances," the "would-be-nice" fixes, you'll burn out before you ever see any results. Focus on the big picture.

Remember this: Big Problems. Big Solutions. Big money.

The Psychology of Pain: Why People Pay for Relief?

Here's a truth most people don't say out loud:

People don't buy products.

They buy *relief.*

They buy an *escape.*

They buy *hope.*

They buy *results.*

If someone's in pain, deep, frustrating, soul-draining pain. In this case, they're not shopping for features or comparing specs. They're looking for the fastest, clearest path out to get immediate relief. And if you can give them that? You've got their full attention. Possibly even their loyalty for a lifetime.

Why?

Because the human brain is wired for survival, not success.

At the most basic level, our brains are designed to avoid pain more urgently than we seek pleasure. It's called the "negativity bias", a built-in radar that's constantly scanning for threats, discomforts, or anything that could feel bad. This isn't just philosophy; it's neuroscience. Pain activates regions in the brain that are tied to focus and urgency. That means, when someone is hurting, they're not distracted. They're alert. They're *ready to act.* They are ready to pay you.

That's why people procrastinate on "important" things like long-term savings or personal growth, but they throw money at a temporary fix when they hit a breaking point.

Ever seen someone buy an overpriced phone charger in an airport because theirs died at the gate? Or order a ride-sharing car just to avoid a 5-minute walk in the rain? That's not rational behaviour, it's relief behaviour. The discomfort became too loud to ignore, and the solution was close enough to touch and buy. Problem solved.

This is what great business people understand.

It's not about building their business, but about how to bring rapid relief to their customers before anyone else in the market.

Your job as a problem-solver isn't just to sell something. It's to enter the pain scene. To understand it, name it, and offer a clear path out of it. The clearer and more emotionally connected your solution is to that pain, the more powerful your impact and your income will be.

Now here's where it gets interesting.

People also pay to avoid *future* pain.

That's why insurance exists.

That's why parents save for college.

That's why people invest in training or coaching, where they want to prevent something painful from happening later in the future.

So you're not just solving present pain, you're easing future anxiety as well. As a result, you're giving them peace of mind.

But for that to work, they have to trust you. They have to believe that you *get it*. That you're not just selling, but serving. And that you've been where they are, or provide that

28

validation to show that you've helped others through their own pain points. In short, you have been there and done that.

The deeper their pain, the deeper your empathy must go.

When people are hurting, they don't just want a solution; they want someone who *understands*. Someone who listens. Someone who offers clarity instead of more confusion. If you become that person who offers real relief, you don't just earn a customer.

You earn influence.

And influence, in today's world, is the most valuable currency there is.

The Three Types of Pain: Personal, Professional, and Societal

Pain doesn't wear the same face. Sometimes it's a whisper in your mind. Other times, it's a punch to the gut. But, in business, it usually appears in three main forms: **personal, professional, and societal**.

And each one holds and showcases its kind of opportunity.

1. Personal Pain

This is the most common and the most emotional.

It lives in the heart, in the habits, and in the quiet moments no one sees.

It's the pain of a single mom who feels overwhelmed by time and responsibility.

It's the twenty-something drowning in self-doubt, wondering if they'll ever "make it."

It's the man who looks in the mirror and sees failure, even though he's trying his best.

29

Personal pain is powerful because it's close.

It's intimate. It affects how someone *feels about themselves*.

And when you touch that, when your solution eases that burden, you're not just helping.

You're healing them from the inside.

That's why many personal development coaches, fitness instructors, mental health advocates, and spiritual guides have thriving businesses raking in millions of dollars each year.

They help people feel *whole* again. Or even for the first time in their lives.

If your idea makes someone's life lighter, clearer, and more meaningful, you're in the business of transformation. And that's a business that never goes out of style and will stay evergreen.

2. Professional Pain

This type of pain hits where it hurts, and it hits in the workplace, careers, and ambitions.

It's the overwhelmed employee who can't keep up with tasks. The frustrated freelancer who can't find high-paying clients. The entrepreneur who is buried in systems they don't understand.

Professional pain is often easier to monetise because people are already conditioned to pay for performance.

They'll invest in tools, training, or services if it helps them do their job better or achieve faster results.

This is why B2B (business-to-business) solutions are so profitable.

You're not just selling to a person, you're problem-solving for a mission, and most likely, it may save an entire organization from financial ruin. A goal. A bottom line.

Want to help a company save time? Great.

Want to help them make money, retain staff, or close more deals? Even better.

When your offer solves *professional pain*, your pricing can scale fast because the ROI is tangible. And most importantly, those businesses will be willing to pay you top dollars to get top results.

3. Societal Pain

This one is big. Heavy. And often messy.

It's the pain that affects *groups* of people, not just individuals.

It's inequality. Injustice. Healthcare gaps. Educational barriers. Climate anxiety. Systemic dysfunction.

Societal pain is often the most complex to solve, but it's also where world-changing businesses are born.

Think about companies that built their brand around helping underserved communities. Or platforms that give voice to the voiceless. Or tech that democratizes access to resources.

These businesses don't just chase profit. They chase *progress*.

And in doing so, they often earn the deepest kind of loyalty.

But here's the thing: you don't have to be a billionaire or run a non-profit to solve societal pain.

You just have to care. And take action in your corner of the world. Focus on your locale and expand outwards.

You can build a tutoring app that lifts kids out of failing schools.

Create a course that helps first-generation entrepreneurs understand money.

Design an experience that gives marginalised voices a safe place to be heard.

Because solving pain isn't always about scale, it's about *service*.

Now here's the question:

Which kind of pain are you best at solving?

You don't have to choose all of the above scenarios.

Start with the one that stirs your heart. The one that moves you.

Because passion fuels persistence, and persistence is what brings results.

How to Measure the Size of a Problem?

Not every problem is worth solving. That might sound harsh, but it's true.

Some problems are just *inconveniences*. Others? They're life-altering obstacles that stop people in their tracks.

If you want to build a business that scales and lasts, you've got to learn how to measure the **weight** of a problem.

Solving *any* problem won't make you wealthy. Solving a *big* one might.

So, what makes a problem "big"?

1. Frequency: How Often Does It Happen?
A one-time annoyance might get a shrug.

But a recurring frustration? That's where tension builds, ripples outward, and affects everyone in its path. It must be stopped now and at all costs.

It builds emotional pressure over time if someone struggles with something daily or weekly.

It becomes a constant drain. And the more they feel it, the more desperate they are for a fix.

For example:

A website glitch that crashes once a year? Annoying, but tolerable. But one that happens every time they try to check out while shopping? That's a revenue killer. *That* problem needs to get solved fast, and now, the person who specialises in solving it gets paid whatever he or she demands.

The more frequent the pain, the more urgent the relief.

2. Intensity: How Bad Does It Feel?

Some problems are loud. Some are subtle. But intensity isn't just about noise, it's about impact.

Does the problem cause embarrassment? Does it waste money?

Does it threaten someone's job, confidence, or well-being?

If the answer is yes, you're looking at high-intensity pain. That's the kind of pain that makes someone say, *"I'll do anything to fix this."*

A parent watching their child struggle in school.

A business is losing thousands due to a software error.

An individual is buried in shame because of a personal failure.

These aren't casual problems.

They hit hard at the weakest points at the most unexpected time, and people don't just want a solution; they *need* it fast, meaning right now.

3. Scale: How Many People Are Affected?

Even if a problem is deep and frequent, one more thing must be truly valuable: **reach**.

You might have the perfect solution to a niche frustration, but your income has a ceiling if only 17 people worldwide have that issue.

That's not to say niche solutions can't thrive; they absolutely or possibly may.

But the bigger the pool of people affected by a problem, the larger your solution becomes.

For instance:

Helping teenagers overcome social anxiety? Huge market.

Helping new freelancers onboard clients more easily? Still a great niche.

Helping left-handed underwater basket weavers file taxes? Probably not your goldmine.

So when you're evaluating a problem, ask:

- Does it happen often?
- Does it cause real frustration or harm?
- Are a lot of people dealing with it?

If you answer "yes" to all three, you're holding a diamond.

And here's one final filter that simplifies it all:

Would someone pay for this?
Not in theory. But today. Right now. With urgency. In reality.

If they did, you don't just have an idea.

You have a solution the market wants. And that's where every great business begins.

The Emotional Multiplier: When a Small Problem Feels Huge

Not every problem looks big on the outside. Some are tiny, quiet, barely visible to others. But to the person living with it? It's massive. That's the emotional multiplier at work. You see, logic measures problems by size. Emotion measures problems by *weight*. And what feels heavy, heavy will always matter more than what looks big.

Let me give you an example.

A man gets home after a long day, and the TV remote is missing.

Small problem, right?

But if his entire day has been a mess, his boss yelled, traffic sucked, bank account's low, this little missing remote might be the final straw. He snaps. He yells. He throws something.

Why?

Because the emotional context of a problem makes it grow much larger than it is.

Here's another example that plays out every day in the business world:

A young entrepreneur spends months creating a product. Launch day comes, and nobody buys. It's not just a failed offer; it *feels* like a failed identity. They spiral. Not because one launch defines their worth, but because they've attached their *entire value* to its outcome.

Now, to someone else? That might look like no big deal. "Try again," they'll say.

But when you're emotionally invested and've wrapped your confidence or hope around something, even a small setback can feel like a major collapse.

This is where problem-solvers thrive.

Because the opportunity isn't always in fixing the *size* of the problem, it's in addressing how big it feels.

Think about some of the most successful products and services around you. Many of them don't solve massive societal issues. They simply solve *emotionally loud* ones.

- Meditation apps that help anxious people calm down before bed.

- Tools that help creators avoid the shame of posting content that flops.

- Courses that help new parents feel like they aren't failing.

- Fashion advice that helps someone feel confident on a first date.

Small moments. Big feelings.

That's the power of perception.

And it's your job to tune into it.

Because when you build empathy into your business, when you ask, *"What's going on underneath this?"* you stop treating customers like data points and start treating them like humans. You will get to know them and understand their true needs.

And humans are emotional creatures.

They remember how you made them feel far more than what you sold them.

So here's the play:

Look for small annoyances that carry big emotional weight.

Listen for moments when people say things like:

- "I know it's silly, but this bothers me…"
- "I shouldn't be this upset, but I can't help it…"
- "It's just a little thing, but it ruins my whole day…"

Those are clues.

Clues that a small fix might mean the *world* to someone out there. And many small fixes are waiting to be solved by you. The catch is that you will need to know where to look for them first. Then to act on them.

And when you become the person who solves problems and feels-sized problems, your value skyrockets.

Not because you're flashy.

But because you're *felt*.

Hidden Pains: The Gold Under the Surface

Some of the most profitable problems in the world don't get shouted.

They get *silenced*.

These are the hidden pains.

The quiet struggles people don't post about.

The ones they don't have language for.

The ones people carry for years, sometimes without even realising it's a problem, until someone shows them it can be fixed.

If you want to build a business that truly connects, one that *feels necessary* to your audience, learn how to spot what others overlook.

Here's the secret:

The best problem-solvers don't just listen to what people say.

They listen to what people *mean*.

They look between the words. They study the tone. They feel the energy behind someone's frustration.

Because let's be honest, most people don't know how to describe what's wrong.

They'll say, "I'm always tired and do not know why."

But the pain might be that they feel invisible at work or unappreciated at home.

They'll say, "I need to get organized."

But maybe they're overwhelmed because their boundaries are broken, not their to-do list.

They'll say, "I'm stuck in life and lost. And I need help." That is their silent cry for attention.

And beneath that is a cocktail of fear, shame, and uncertainty they've never unpacked.

The pain is real. But it's *hidden*.

And that's your opportunity.

When you build a business around **unspoken pain**, you do something rare:

You create *felt understanding*.

And that creates trust.

Think of the businesses that have quietly exploded over the last decade.

- Journaling apps that help people process emotions in private.

- Personal finance platforms that speak to people who grew up never learning about money.

- Body-positive clothing brands that don't just sell clothes—but sell confidence.

- Therapy services that normalize asking for help without shame.

These businesses thrive because they don't just target problems. They target pain that's been hiding in plain sight.

They see what others miss.

And that's where real loyalty is born, not just customer interest, but an *emotional connection.*

So how do you uncover hidden pain?

You listen.

You ask better questions.

You observe when people laugh nervously, dodge a topic, or downplay something that matters.

You follow patterns of behavior.

You notice the workarounds people use, the awkward silences, the "this is fine" moments that *aren't fine.*

You get curious.

You get empathetic.

And most of all—you stay human.

Because the person who *feels* the pain best is the one who solves it best.

And when you reflect on someone's struggle and connect to them with clarity and kindness, you become more than a business. You become a *bridge* from confusion to clarity, suffering to relief.

People remember that. They also appreciate it wholeheartedly.

They share that with others, and that's how your business has the potential to scale to the top. It's also when your business doesn't just grow. It becomes *needed*.

Market Validation: How to Know if It's a "Big" Problem?

You've found a pain. Maybe even a hidden one. It feels deep. It feels important.

But here's the next question that separates dreamers from doers: **Is anyone else feeling it too?**

Because in business, it's not enough to believe in a problem.

You need to **validate** it.

You need evidence that it's real, pressing, and people are willing to *pay* for a solution.

Validation is how you save yourself from building a beautiful solution to a problem nobody cares enough to solve.

So, how do you validate?

Start with this: Evidence lives in emotion and behavior.

1. Search for Signals
Go where people complain.

That's your goldmine.

Look through public forums in the comments section.

Search for keywords related to your idea and see what people are saying.

Are they frustrated? Are they confused? Are they begging for help? Where are they lacking, and what are their pain points?

You've likely uncovered a real pain point if you see repeated frustration across multiple people in different places.

Now dig deeper:

- Are people actively searching for solutions on various search engines?

- Are there products or services already trying to help, but are doing it poorly?

- Are customers leaving negative reviews saying, "I wish this did more than what the advertisement said..."?

That's not the competition you need to be afraid of. You need to focus on the unmet needs waiting to be met and the voids that need to be filled.

That's proof and validation to show that *money is already flowing there*. You just have to do it better. Much better than them.

2. Talk to Real People
Validation becomes clearer when you stop guessing and start asking.

Ask your audience, your peers, your past customers, your network:

"What's the biggest frustration you have with ___?"

"What have you tried to fix it with?"

"What would a perfect solution look like to you?"

You're not selling yet. You're listening. You're learning. You're gathering insights that data can't give you.

You're looking for **patterns**.

Because if ten people describe the same problem in ten different ways?

You've just struck something powerful: a common pain wrapped in different languages.

That's market-ready.

3. Look for their Willingness to Pay

And now, the test that matters most:

Will someone *pay* to make this pain go away?

It doesn't matter how much they complain.

What matters is: Are they willing to spend money to have it fixed?

You're in business if they're already investing in tools, coaching, books, software, or shortcuts.

If they're just venting and tolerating the pain with no action? Maybe they are not ready yet.

So now is the time to test it.

Put together a quick version of your solution, package it, and offer it to the open market.

See if people sign up. If they don't, talk to them again. Learn as to why. Adjust accordingly. Then, make a Reoffer that takes a different approach by having them focus on the results. Results and benefits are what they are looking for. People look for what's in it for them.

Because the only way to know if you've got something valuable is to take it to the people in pain—and see if they say yes.

That "yes" is the difference between a guess and a goldmine.

Why Big Pain Equals Big Money?

Let's wrap up this chapter with a truth you *can't afford* to ignore:

The more pain you relieve, the more money you can ethically and realistically make.

It's that simple.

But it's also that powerful.

This isn't about manipulation. It's not about taking advantage of people.

It's about giving them *value*.

And in the marketplace, value is defined by the size, depth, and urgency of the problem you solve.

If you relieve the minor inconveniences, you will get a minor income.

Do you relieve deep-seated pain affecting someone's life, confidence, or livelihood? Now, you earn the permission to charge **real** money.

Let's look at an example.

Say you sell a basic to-do list app. Cool. But there are hundreds of free ones out there.

Now imagine you create a system that helps burned-out executives delegate 30% of their workload, recover 10 hours a week, and finally spend time with their families again.

That's no longer a to-do app. That's a *life upgrade*.

That's worth hundreds—maybe thousands of dollars—to the right person.

Why?

Because you're not just selling features. You're delivering **relief**.

And people pay more when the outcome feels like a **transformation**.

Let's flip it again:

A $20 wrist brace may help someone with mild wrist strain, which may offer some temporary relief.

But if a surgeon comes along and offers a $150,000 procedure to *permanently remove* the pain that has been keeping you from working or sleeping, you will be ready to pay for it.

It's because of the impact and the permanent relief from suffering that the surgery may potentially offer.

The more intense the pain, the more urgent the need.

The more urgent the need, the higher the perceived value.

And the higher the perceived value, the more premium pricing you can ethically charge.

Big pain = Big money.

But here's the key word: **ethically**.

You're not tricking people into buying anything.

You're not creating false urgency.

You're solving something *real*.

You're showing up with skill, compassion, and proven results.

That's the difference between a "hustler" and a true entrepreneur.

Real entrepreneurs don't chase attention.

They chase *solutions*.

They chase outcomes.

They build things that work and earn a big income because they can create a big enough *impact and deliver big solutions to big problems*.

And when you solve something that deeply matters, something that's been costing someone their sleep, sanity, or sense of self, you'll not only get paid, you'll be remembered.

So stop trying to outsmart.

Stop obsessing over trendy features or pretty branding. Focus on giving results by fine-tuning your skills.

Start by asking:

- Where does it hurt?
- How deep does it go?
- What would change and how would they feel if I fixed this for someone?

Because that's your power.

That's your leverage.

That's your path to creating income, influence, freedom, and legacy.

Big money isn't in selling harder.

It's in *solving anything much better*.

And now, you know exactly where to start. Go for it and make it happen.

CHAPTER 2

Where Do Big Problems Hide?
What to Look For and Where?

Big problems don't wear name tags. They don't approach you and say, "Hi, I'm the next billion-dollar idea." They're hidden in the cracks, the chaos, and the everyday complaints.

They're buried under habits. Tangled in inefficiencies. Lost in outdated systems, broken processes, and industries that haven't evolved in decades.

And if you're waiting for someone to point them out to you, you will be waiting for a very long time, and you will miss them.

Because, by the time the problem is obvious to *everyone*, it's already being solved by *someone else*.

The trick isn't just to look harder.

It's to *look smarter*.

To see what others overlook.

To listen to what others talk about.

To ask, "Why is this still being done this way?", "Is there a better and cheaper way to do this?" and mean it wholeheartedly.

That's where big problems hide. And that's where your opportunity begins.

1. Hidden in Plain Sight

Let's start with something that may surprise you: The biggest problems don't usually need discovery. They need *recognition*. They're not tucked away in secret labs or buried inside classified files. They're everywhere. In hospitals. In schools. In public transportation. In meetings. In workplaces. In software. In kitchens. In bedrooms.

But people have gotten used to the broken system, and they have adapted to it. They may have tried to rectify the dysfunctional issue, but may not have found a solution to the problem. After a few tries, they may have given up altogether until you come along with a solution in hand. Now they are thrilled to know about it and learn more.

People have normalized dysfunction. Many have even given up trying to change the system. Red tape, bureaucracy, and other hurdles may be preset barriers to entry.

They begin to accept "the way things are" at face value because they believe that they don't have the power to change anything.

That's where *you* come in.

You're not just looking for trends. You're looking for tension and abnormalities.

You're looking for that moment when someone says:

- "This is so frustrating."
- "There's got to be a better way."
- "I hate doing it this way."
- "Why hasn't anyone fixed this yet?"
- "Is there a faster, easier, and cheaper way to get this thing done right the first time?"

Those aren't complaints.

They're *breadcrumbs*.

Follow them. And it will lead you to their problems. To get started, be a keen observer with an ability to listen and be patient.

For example:

People were tired of standing in the rain trying to catch a cab. So, ridesharing companies started showing up. All they did was find a problem people were facing and found a solution to fix it by connecting two parties and getting the problem solved. They do not own their cars, manage, or maintain them.

This may have created many jobs in the process, and on the other hand, many may have lost their jobs too in the same sector. We live in a disruptive era where the new finds a way to replace the outdated. This brings in new ideas and innovation to the center stage and the forefront. This sparks imagination and creativity to help solve chronically outdated problems.

People were frustrated waiting all day for a package delivery with a window of time stretching a few hours. The big box stores found a way to solve that. Delivery time to your doorstep is an hour or less. This involves a lot of planning, logistics, and automation behind the scenes, sequencing the routes, and communicating between various departments. It may seem simple from a customer's perspective, but a lot is happening behind the scenes that the customer is unaware of. They do not even give it a thought.

When people started hating their overpriced gym memberships, a disruptor appeared on stage and found a way to bring workouts into homes and onto apps. This way, you could work out in your home at your leisure and for free. People are finally wanting change, and technology has helped transform our society and our lives for the better. Gone are the days of the travel agent. These days, you have become one yourself. You can be on a flight in two hours and fly out at any time of the day or night. Everything is available at your disposal and at your beck and call. You get the point.

These weren't new frustrations.

They were just *finally solved* in ways that made sense. If someone had not solved them yet, we would still be complaining about our lives in the old-fashioned and outdated ways.

You're not here to invent pain or invent anything new.

You're here to relieve pain that has existed for many years and has never been solved, maybe because it wasn't profitable for others. But it might be profitable for you. Pain has always been here and will be here forever. But if you can provide relief that feels fresh, easy, cheap, intuitive, and meaningful, you will be raking in money round the clock.

2. Inside Broken Systems

Whenever you deal with a clunky interface, an outdated policy, or a "we've always done it this way" culture, you're looking at a system ripe for disruption. And you may be the person the World is waiting for. Yes, you. Why not you?

Big problems love to hide inside big systems:

- Education and Financial Illiteracy
- Disease and Healthcare
- Transportation and Lack of
- Government and Corruption
- Finance and Ones Barely making it
- Real Estate and Homelessness
- Logistics and Excess Luggage

49

- Traditional media and Manipulation

- Energy and Minimal utilization of renewables

- Small Businesses and lack of scalability

- Scarcity and Poverty

- Hunger and Food

- Fashion and Mass market

- Luxury and Mediocre Stuff

These systems often run on slow-moving structures, obsolete models, and are usually layered in bureaucracy.

They usually tend to resist change. And that makes them perfect hunting grounds for innovators. There may be opportunities lurking in here for the person who has the vision and the mission to bring about change.

Let's talk about healthcare for a moment.

In many parts of the world, booking a doctor's appointment is a tedious process, often with long hold times, hours of waiting, confusing insurance paperwork, and unpredictable costs that become a financial burden to many patients and their families.

Why is it so? Why can't it be just like any other business? You pay a set price for the service, as you would when you service your car and pay the mechanic or hire a plumber. Why does the healthcare industry need a middleman, such as insurance companies, to form a barrier between doctors and patients? And who gets to dictate the treatment for the patient? You know the answer to that.

This may be your opportunity to be a disruptor in this field. Look around you, and you will spot many more opportunities that await disruption. They stay hidden, in the darkness and silence, waiting to be unleashed.

This may be because the system may not be designed with *patients* in mind, but for the profits of these *institutions* that run them. We see this play out every day.

And when a system forgets the human element it's supposed to serve, a massive opportunity is born. There, you may have an opportunity waiting to be solved.

If you can make something simpler, smoother, faster, economical, or more humane, you've got a product people will pay for.

So here's a question you need to start asking every time you deal with a system:

"What part of this process is filled with wasted time, drained energy, one that is filled with inefficiencies and paperwork, or one that is confusing?" That area may be ripe for an overhaul or disruption.

That's where big problems hide.

And the person who fixes even a *small* part of this *big* system?

They don't just earn money.

They earn trust. Influence. And sometimes, market dominance through disruption.

3. In Between Generations
Every generation brings with it a new way of thinking.

A new set of expectations. A new demand for how things should work.

And when that demand crashes into the reality of how things *currently* work, guess what appears?

A gap. A problem. A pain APPEARS.

And inside that pain lives *opportunity*.

Millennials, for instance, grew up watching their parents buy houses, work one job for life, and retire with a pension. That model no longer exists.

Now they graduate facing massive student loan debt, job market uncertainty, and a place where they feel stuck, unable to make money at a job or move up the rungs of societal and familial expectations, and putting a roof over their head. And inflation is not making it any easier for them either.

Boom. Market pain. That's a bundle of pain waiting to be challenged and solved.

The thought process for Gen Z is filled with digital fluency, having less patience for friction, and a deep-seated desire for transparency, values, and community.

They don't want to accumulate products, be tied to a home, or be stuck with a car payment similar to that of the previous generations. Instead, they seek *movement, freedom, minimalism, and experiences. They become renters.*

They want brands they can believe in. They seek to buy the best and hold them forever.

Any business still operating with a 1900s mentality will go under without a fight. They will soon become obsolete and die out without a trace. They will succumb to their obsolescence. They will need to adapt fast to survive modern times, where things are moving fast and demand immediate results.

But this generational clash also creates space for problem-solvers.

See for yourself how many social media platforms have exploded by providing space for user-generated content (UGC), since the younger generation sought a platform to showcase expression, speed, and visibility, not curated feeds and old-school algorithms.

It's how fintech apps found momentum because traditional banking felt slow, rigid, and disconnected from modern times.

If you can see where generations collide, you'll be able to see where industries are forced to evolve.

What happens if you can meet the *new expectations* faster than the incumbents?

Then you win.

4. Emerging Trends: How Shifts in Behavior Reveal Problems?

The world is always changing, but most people are too busy reacting to notice what those changes mean.

As a problem-solver, your job isn't just to spot the change.

It's to spot the *friction* that comes with it.

Because every new trend, whether cultural, technological, social, or economic, *creates a wave of problems*.

Let's break them down.

When the advent of remote work exploded, the initial reaction was excitement: freedom, flexibility, and not having to commute. Just rolling out of bed and working in pajamas would have been a luxury.

But, behind that freedom came *frustration*: poor home office setups, video call fatigue, team misalignment, decreased productivity, loss of human connection, loneliness, depression, and burnout.

That created a fresh layer of needs:

- Software for asynchronous teams
- Mental health platforms for remote workers
- Ergonomic furniture brands

- Virtual coworking communities

All of these were built not because remote work was a new idea, but because it suddenly became *everyone's* reality, and people weren't prepared.

The trend exposed the pain.

This happens constantly, and it's happening now as you read this book.

When financial literacy became mainstream, people suddenly wanted financial education, wallets, tracking tools, and tax help.

Today, AI has taken over our lives and is available to everyone who wishes to change the World for the better. As a result, we need prompt engineers, ethics consultants, integration apps, and regulatory interpreters. Those positions have never existed before in history.

Plant-based diets are gaining popularity, grocery stores need better labeling, restaurants need new menus, and consumers need clear nutritional guidance.

Following the pattern, we see that the trend is to go in this sequence:

Trend → Adoption → Confusion → Need → Business Opportunity

So, when watching the news, scrolling through social media, or getting a sneak peek of the currently trending fads, don't just ask, *"What's new?"*

Ask yourself, how can I find the gap in the marketplace and fill it with my solution to people's problems?

- *"What's confusing people about this?"*
- *"What problems are currently trending?"*

- *"What are the evergreen problems waiting to be solved?"*

- *What are the multigenerational problems that exist today, and how can I disrupt that sequence?*

- *"What's overwhelming about this shift in change?"*

- *"What's not keeping up with this new demand?"*

The earlier you see the need, the less competition you'll face.

The sooner you act, the faster you can become the go-to name in that space.

Because here's the deal: trends are flashy.

But behind every flash, there's a *shadow of friction*.

Solve the friction—not just the flash—and you'll win long after the trend fades.

5. The "Boring" Industries with Billion-Dollar Gaps

Everyone wants to build the next hot thing.

But you know where the real money is?

In the boring stuff. Boring businesses that are underappreciated and underrecognized.

I'm talking about:

- Accounting
- Warehousing
- Plumbing
- Logistics
- Supply chains
- Waste management
- Payroll compliance

55

- Parking enforcement
- Construction scheduling
- Trade businesses
- Online Subscriptions

These industries aren't the next shiny object or are sexy, but they're often full of outdated tools, frustrated users, and massive inefficiencies.

Because here's the truth: when an industry is "boring," it means fewer entrepreneurs are trying to disrupt it.

That means *less noise.*

And less noise means *more opportunity* for anyone bold enough to look and act on it before the word gets out and attracts the crowd.

Let's look at an example.

Many online payment processors didn't become multi-billion-dollar companies because they made something cool.

They became giants by solving just one annoying, universal pain: online payments were too complicated for developers. When something complex is made much simpler and user-friendly, things take shape and growth happens.

Those companies made it simple. Fast and Clean.

They didn't chase a lifestyle trend.

They solved a *technical bottleneck,* one that millions of businesses faced daily: the Collection of payments.

Or consider some software companies that made site management a breeze through their proprietary software. One successful company that benefited from its use is a construction software company that built tools to make project management easier for job sites.

Not glamorous.

But vital.

Boring industries are *essential industries*. That's why they have *predictable money*. Budgets. Contracts. Repeat customers. High stakes. The average consumer may not know their name, but those businesses do exist in the limelight. They are also hiding in plain sight.

These are the businesses that need you, and you need them? You will be paying them each month and each year. Rain or shine, stock market crash, a recession, or when everything is at its peak. And you will keep paying them, and they will be raking in their profits, scaling their company, and remaining evergreen. They may also be in their best financial position to buy others out.

So ask yourself:

- What's something that people *need*, even if they don't talk about it?
- What's an industry that's been doing things the same way since the early 1900s?
- What's something that sounds boring but drives billions in economic value?

That's your angle.

That's your niche.

That's your edge.

Stop chasing glamour.

Start chasing *problems no one else wants to touch*.

Because when you fix what's "boring," you build something unshakable. It may even outlive you and can help you create generational wealth for your family.

6. Where Money Moves: Follow the Spending to Find Pain

Here's a universal principle that never fails:

"Money flows where pain lives."

If you want to find problems, follow the money. Big problems, big money. Take note of where people are spending and for what.

And more specifically, follow *people where they are already spending to fix things that are broken*. You do not need to reinvent the wheel or invent something new. Just follow the above concept, which is basic to its core.

Even if the solution sucks, and people are willing to spend time fixing it, it says a lot more about the problem. This means the problem is *real and there is plenty of money to be made*.

And that's your cue.

Look at where people are already dropping cash:

- Courses they don't finish
- Subscriptions that they forget to cancel
- Products they use only once, and then they sit collecting dust
- Services that kind of help but don't go all the way
- Agencies that promise a lot but deliver very little

Every dollar spent on a half-solution is a signal that someone is *still hurting*.

Still looking.

Still unsatisfied.

You don't need to convince them they have a problem; they already know that they have one.

Your job is to offer a better, clearer, simpler, and more honest answer. Once you help them solve their problem from start to finish, they will stay as your ambassadors to your brand for life. And they will help you market your company for free and advertise your product. They may even say how you solved their problems on social media, which may bring you a loyal virtual following. It may even have the potential to become a worldwide event. You may never know.

This is also true in B2B.

Look at where companies spend tons of money on training, consultants, and new software.

Ask: "Are they getting what they are paying for?"

If the answer is no or even "sort of," that's an *opening*.

"Money talks. But wasted money screams."

Follow the flow.

And position yourself as the *upgrader*, the *fixer*, the person to provide *clarity* amidst the chaos.

You don't have to create a market from scratch.

You just have to do what others are doing, but much *better*.

7. The Underground Economy of Frustration

If you want to find a hidden opportunity, stop chasing inspiration and start chasing *irritation*.

Because where people are quietly frustrated, there's a quiet market opening.

And that market is *begging* for help.

I call this the underground economy of frustration, where people want to get their problems solved behind the scenes. In DMs. In group chats. In the side forums and the dark corners of the internet. They're venting, complaining, hacking,

59

improvising, and silently hoping someone will *finally* help build the thing that will make their life easier.

These frustrations rarely show up in mainstream surveys or polished feedback forms or in 5-star reviews. They live in:

- Private channels
- Niche communications
- Site reviews
- Comment sections
- Community groups
- Internal spreadsheets and in systems nobody's proud of

People are used to patching together solutions with duct tape and sheets. They're juggling browser extensions and copy-paste routines.

They're whispering, "Ugh, I hate this part of my job," under their breath.

And here's the gold: they'll never *ask* for a solution…

But they'll instantly recognize it when they see one.

Let's say you're targeting digital creators. Everyone is building tools for content calendars and social media scheduling these days. They are plentiful. In reality, these creators aren't just struggling with scheduling; they're drowning in *mental fatigue* from decision-making, idea generation, and engagement anxiety.

That's not obvious.

But it's real.

It lives in late-night texts, not in business dashboards.

If you can tap into that sector of people who have that kind of pain-friction, who feel it but don't verbalize, you become the person who "just gets it."

And those businesses? They don't need to shout.

Once you help them solve their pain points, these customers will whisper your name to others.

They will say, "He or she is the one. He or she finally fixed it for me."

That's the power of solving underground frustrations.

You don't just create a tool. You create *relief* and instant *trust*. More so, a loyal customer for life.

8. How to Train Your Eyes to See Hidden Problems?

Seeing problems isn't a gift; it's a skill.

And like any other skill, it can be sharpened. But it will need to be learned first.

Here's how you can become the person who sees opportunity where others see nothing:

a. Listen with Curiosity, Not Confirmation

Most people listen to respond. You need to listen to *understand*.

Instead of offering advice right away, dig in. Ask the right questions:

- "Tell me more about that."
- "Why was that frustrating?"
- "What would a better version of that look like?"

Then wait. Let people vent. In their venting lives, the truth. And the truth will always surface.

b. Keep a "Problem Notebook."

Every time you hear or experience friction, write it down.

Whether it's a glitch in an app, a line too long at a store, or a policy that makes no sense—log it in your notebook.

Over time, your notebook becomes a treasure map of possible solutions.

c. Become a Student of Patterns

Notice where complaints overlap.

If three business owners tell you that their onboarding clients are a nightmare...

If four parents tell you they hate packing school lunches...

If five contractors say invoicing takes too long...

Pay attention. They are venting their frustrations at anyone patient enough to listen to them. That's a pattern worth pursuing.

d. When You Experience the Frustration Yourself

Don't just read reviews. You will need to experience it firsthand to understand it.

What happens when you see something broken and need it fixed, and can't get someone to fix it right away? You try to do it yourself, right? When you try the clunky tool and find it is not designed for that job, you start looking for other options. What happens when you try to navigate through a system filled with inefficiency, red tape, and bureaucracy? More frustrations.

When you *feel* the pain, you start designing with empathy, not ego.

Empathy is the most valuable design skill.

9. Becoming the Translator Positioned Between Pain and Profit

Here's the final leap most people never make:

They find the pain.

But they don't know how to translate it into a solution.

And even when they build a solution, they don't know how to communicate it in a way that feels urgent and valuable.

That's where *translation* comes in.

You're not just building something useful but bridging the emotional and practical gap.

Let's say you build a budgeting app.

You could say: "Helps you track your spending."

Boring.

Or… you could say: "Finally stop feeling anxious every time you check your bank balance and use it to create your monthly budget."

That's a translation. It's how you package it, say it, and present it.

You're taking the *practical fix* and tying it to the *emotional relief.*

Or if you run a service that automates boring client tasks…

Instead of saying: "Save 10 hours a week."

Try saying: "Finally get your evenings back with ease."

The goal is to make people say, "That's exactly what I've been looking for, even though I didn't know how to say it."

When you do that well, you don't need to sell hard.

The solution speaks for itself, because the pain has already *primed the buyer into making that purchase.*

So here's your job:

1. Identify a specific problem.

2. Understand the emotional *and* practical sides of it.

3. Build a clear, focused solution.

4. Describe it in a way that speaks to the *felt need*, not just the feature.

5. Educate your customers by showing them the results they can expect from your products or services. You may not even need to say a word. A live demo can help say it all.

Do that consistently, and your ideas will stop feeling like products.

They will give your customers a good feeling, a feeling filled with the *answers they are looking for.*

And answers, when packaged and executed right, will help sell anything.

THE DISPARITY IN WEALTH

CHAPTER 3

How to Spot Gold in Chaos, Waste, Frustration, and Inefficiencies?

Let's start with a shift in perspective. Most people run from chaos. They check out when things get noisy, messy, unpredictable, or inconvenient. They complain. They wait for someone else to fix the irritant. But entrepreneurs, the real kind, who build things that matter, don't run from chaos.

Entrepreneurs run toward it. Because chaos isn't just noise, it's a signal. A signal that tells them something is broken. That something isn't working. And where something isn't working, value is waiting to be created.

That's the secret. Chaos isn't a curse. It's a clue. It's where unmet needs live. It's where customer frustrations fester. It's where old systems start to fall apart. And in those cracks and breakdowns is where you get to build your empire. That's where you can create something useful, meaningful, and wildly profitable.

Consider this: every major innovation we admire today was born out of someone's frustration with how things were, and has not changed in the last 100 years. Homes in exotic vacation spots emerged out of nowhere and were made available to tourists because travelers were sick of overpriced, impersonal hotel rooms. Sharing rides was created to solve the chaos of unreliable taxi service.

Online product order deliveries were built to cut through the friction of limited inventory and exhausting store visits. These weren't inventions out of thin air; they were, in fact, solutions to real chaos. Look in your vicinity, and you may find opportunities lurking in the shadows that can help you be in the ranks of billionaires.

The founders behind these businesses didn't wait for things to calm down. They may have wanted it to stay turbulent so they could capitalize on the confusion and inconveniences of others. They didn't look for perfect markets because they know that perfection does not exist.

They looked at broken systems and asked themselves, "If I'm this annoyed, how many other people may be feeling the same?" And, they worked on finding a solution, and then came the answer.

This is how great businesses are born: not from theory but tension. Real-world tension. The stuff you feel in your gut when you think, "There's got to be a better way." Most people ignore that feeling. But you're not most people. You're a builder. A fixer. A problem-solver. Your job is to pay attention to that frustration and lean into it.

Let's get even more specific. Chaos reveals itself in many forms: slow apps, long lines, clunky systems, outdated policies, red tape and bureaucracy, and confusing processes. Every time something breaks, stalls, or wastes your time, you've got a window open into a much bigger issue. And that issue might be your opportunity to open up and offer a helping hand with solutions.

Think about this: Frustration is a sign of demand without a readily available supply. When people complain, "This is so annoying," "This takes too long," "Why is this still being done this way?" what they're saying is: "I want this to be much easier. I want this to be better. And I'm willing to pay for a solution." That's demand. Emotional demand, sure, but all that we spend on is purely emotional.

This is why frustration should excite you. It's raw, it's real, and it's rarely wrong. It doesn't hide behind market research or perfectly polished surveys. It pours out in late-night rants, social media threads, and with eye-rolls around the dinner table. It's the real data you'll ever get. These are analogous to the boots on the ground. That's hardcore real-life experience that is being tested.

Now, let's talk about another goldmine hiding within the midst of chaos: Waste. Wasted time. Wasted energy. Wasted resources. Wasted attention. Waste is everywhere, and most people have learned to live with it. And have considered it as the norm. But what about you? You should see it for what it is—a map to wealth. Don't you see opportunity lurking inside it by now? Waste is your red flag. Every inefficient system is a doorway to innovation. Every repeated task that sucks up time, resources, and energy is a sign that automation, delegation, and redesign are needed. And the one who steps in to fix that? That's the person who gets paid top dollars.

For example, imagine a business spending thousands of dollars per month on support calls to get simple answers to the same five questions from customers. That's not "normal." That's a leak. And a smart problem-solver would plug that leak with better onboarding, clearer instructions, or even a chatbot. Think of an employee who copies and pastes from one system to another and spends about three hours daily to complete it. That's not supposed to be "It is just how it is," or " It's how it works here." That's a drain on productivity, which is screaming for automation.

It's not only seen in businesses, either. Individuals also waste their most precious resources: mental energy and time.

Examples may include: A Student using five different apps to study. Mom is juggling disconnected tools to manage her household. A Freelancer is buried in emails because he or she cannot find a better client system. These people aren't lazy or unmotivated. They're drowning in cluttered systems not built with their needs in mind. And they'll gladly pay for something that brings them simplicity and peace of mind.

That brings us to **inefficiency**. If waste is a leak, inefficiency is friction. It's when effort and results don't match. When people try their best and still fall short of their expectations, it may be because of an inefficient system or a malfunctioning software program that does not meet its intended purpose. Inefficiency thrives in outdated forms, hard-to-follow dashboards, and in the 12-step processes that should take only two steps.

Most people don't question inefficiency. They shrug and say, "That's just how it is." In that case, what would be your take on it? I am sure you're here to challenge that. Am I right? Would you ask hard and practical questions? Why does this take so long? Why are people jumping through so many hoops? Why hasn't anyone streamlined this?

Because inefficiency is an open invitation. It's a handwritten note from the market saying: "Fix me, and I'll reward you." People love it when things work better. They stay loyal to what makes life easier for them. And they will be more than happy to refer others to people who help fix the friction in their lives.

You don't need to be flashy to win. You just need to be useful. You need to find the places where friction slows people down and help build bridges for them instead. That's the real power. Not building for attention. But building for *flow*, for momentum, simplicity, and ease.

So don't fear chaos. Don't run from broken systems. Don't look away from inefficiencies that everyone else ignores. That mess you're avoiding? That's your market. That friction you feel? That's your fuel. And the moment you start leaning into the stress, instead of dodging it, dig in and start learning more about it?

That's when the gold will usually tend to show up.

Tracking Emotional Energy: How Feelings Reveal Financial Opportunity?

Emotions are invisible. But they are not powerless. They might be the strongest force in the marketplace. People like to believe that they are making logical decisions. They tend to compare features, prices, and benefits. But underneath all of that is something more primal *feeling*.

The truth is, people don't buy products or services. They buy emotional outcomes. Relief. Confidence. Clarity. Belonging. Peace. Results. When someone pulls out their wallet, they're not just investing in a solution; they're buying a shift in how they feel. If you truly understand that, you'll never run out of opportunities to serve.

So, how do you find these emotional opportunities? You start by tracking energy. Where do people light up with frustration? Where do they shrink in shame? Where do they sigh, roll their eyes, or suddenly get quiet and upset? These moments are not random; they're emotional hotspots. And every hotspot is a sign that a problem takes up precious mental space.

Think of a new mother, overwhelmed by conflicting advice on how to care for her baby. She's sleep-deprived, insecure, and anxious about making mistakes. She's not just looking for baby products; she's also looking for *reassurance* that everything will be OK. If you build a business that gives her confidence, not just tools, she'll stick with you for years.

Or take the example of a startup founder. He's proud, ambitious, and under pressure. He juggles five roles, manages a team, and struggles to get traction. He doesn't just need a consultant—he needs someone who sees him, believes in him, and gives him a sense of control. Your service might help him build systems and processes and provide him with a custom blueprint to steer his business, but the *emotion* you deliver is true empowerment.

When you understand people's feelings, you can design products and offer services geared towards their needs, even when they don't ask for it. You will have that foresight to see what is missing in their needs list and seek to fulfill that need. You will be proactive.

One of the most overlooked skills in entrepreneurship is *emotional listening*. This means going beyond what people say and paying attention to what they *mean*. For example, if someone says, "I just wish I had more time," they're not always discussing time management. They may be talking about exhaustion, lack of support, or hidden guilt. If you take their words at face value, you'll be able to build a basic productivity tool. Instead, if you understand their emotion, you might help create something that changes how they relate to time, self-worth, and energy.

This is where the gold lies. In the layers beneath the words.

Here's something more powerful to remember: most people can't articulate their real problem. They'll be able to describe their symptoms in great depth. "I'm tired." "I'm broke." "I'm confused." "I'm stuck." These all may be surface signals. Your job is to decode them. What's underneath, "I'm tired"? Maybe it's decision fatigue, lack of purpose, or trying to please everyone. What's under, "I'm stuck"? Is it their fear of failure, fear of judgment, or an inner belief that they don't deserve to succeed? When you understand the *emotional engine* behind the complaint, you can engineer a solution that hits the heart, not just the brain.

Great businesses speak to both.

Let's talk about energy. Emotional energy is real. You can feel it in a conversation. In a meeting. In a text. It's either rising or draining you. You've had conversations with someone in the past that may have left you fired up or left you numb. People may feel the same way about products, too. Tools that feel intuitive and empowering raise energy levels. Services that feel out of place, unprofessional, patronizing, or confusing tend to drain energy. And customers may not tell you this directly, but their behaviour will.

This is why design matters. Why tone matters. Why user experience matters. Every part of your offer could add to someone's energy or take it away from them. The best brands don't just solve problems they leave people *feeling better* than they did before. This immediate euphoria of getting something on sale or a deal may give someone a short-term boost to their emotions, but it will soon die down. People may keep spending to keep up with their short-term highs.

If you want to spot business opportunities others miss, follow emotional stress. Look for these patterns:

1. **Avoidance**: Where are people procrastinating or hesitating? That's a sign that something feels emotionally heavy or unclear.

2. **Overcompensation**: Where are people spending too much time, money, and energy on trying to fix something? That's a clue that the real issue hasn't been solved yet.

3. **Embarrassment**: Where do people whisper, hide, go silent, or laugh nervously? That's where shame lives, and people will pay for safe, empowering solutions.

4. **Exhaustion**: Where are people constantly overwhelmed, even when doing something they care about? That's an efficiency or boundary problem, often masked by passion.

Every one of these is a gateway into someone's unspoken need. And when every unspoken need is met with clarity and care, it becomes a foundation for a product, a service, or a brand.

Let's return to a key truth: **money follows energy.** The more emotional energy a person spends on a problem, the more likely they will pay for its relief. The trick is not just recognizing where the energy is being spent but offering a clear path to reclaim it.

So, how do you apply this practically?

Start by asking different questions. Don't just ask, "What's hard for you right now?" Ask, "What drains your energy the most?" Ask, "What do you dread doing, even though it feels necessary?" Ask, "Do you wish someone else to handle it for you?"

Then, listen. Really listen. Write it all down. Don't look for the polished answer you may expect, but look for the moments when emotion breaks through the surface. That's where the real business insight lives.

This process isn't fast. But it's powerful. It creates new businesses when customers feel we have given them the answers they seek. When someone says, "I didn't even know I needed this," that's the highest compliment you can get as an entrepreneur. It means you saw what they didn't. You felt what they didn't have a name for. And you built something that gave them back control, confidence, and calmness.

That's what we're here to do.

So, stop waiting for logical product ideas. Start tracking emotional patterns. Get curious about what people feel, not just what they say. And above all, start paying attention to the energy in every room, every call, every space.

Because if you can spot where the emotional current is surging, you'll know exactly where to lay the foundation for your business empire.

The Power of Micro-Irritations: Small Annoyances with Big Business Potential

Not all pain is dramatic. Not every opportunity comes wrapped in crisis. Sometimes, the gold is in the *micro-irritations*—those small, nagging frustrations that people live with daily and have simply grown used to. They don't complain loudly. They don't boycott or display rage. But they suffer in silence. And every time they sigh, groan, or mutter "this again?" they reveal a gap a tiny crack in the system waiting to be filled by someone bold enough to notice it.

That someone could be you.

Let's define what micro-irritation means. It's a small, repetitive problem that's too minor to be considered a "crisis," but annoying enough to create emotional friction over time. These aren't the disasters or breakdowns, they're the drips. The daily inefficiencies that, when added up, cost people peace, time, or productivity.

Consider these examples:

- The five seconds it takes to wait to skip an ad on a streaming video.

- Having to retype your login info each time a website or password management system doesn't remember you.

- Long dropdown menus with endless country options when signing up for a new app.

- Waiting on hold for customer service with elevator music looping endlessly.

- The five different remotes it takes to operate your home entertainment system.

- Dealing with multiple AI prompts and options when calling a company.

None of these is catastrophic. But they're all mildly annoying. They create friction. And the longer they exist, the more people will have to *tolerate* them, not because they want to, but because they believe, "That's just how it operates." And unfortunately, neither you nor I can do anything about it.

The accepted belief is "that's just how it is." Your open door may be your only open invitation to help solve each of these minor annoyances, which are staring you in the face each day.

Whenever people accept a minor inconvenience as a permanent part of life, they leave room for someone smarter, more curious, and more courageous to offer a better way. That's your opportunity. You must notice what others have normalized and question by challenging the status quo. Why is it so? And what can I do to help change it?

Why does this take fifteen steps instead of just two?

Why hasn't someone simplified this already?

Why is this still being done the way it was done ten years ago?

How can I do it better? What can I bring to the table to make it much faster, efficient, cheaper, and more effective?

Everyone complains, but no one is daring enough to bring about a solution to this common problem. No one is willing to accept that responsibility for a rapid and sustainable solution.

Great businesses are built by people who ask these kinds of questions about things most others ignore.

Think about some of the tools you use daily: Apps that catch typos in real time. Calendars that eliminate the back-and-forth of scheduling meetings. Password management systems, which remember passwords so you don't have to. It may not be a good idea for someone, but it is here for us to use. These tools don't solve "big" problems in the traditional sense. But they help remove *one little source of stress,* and they do it *consistently.* That consistency turns into loyalty. And that loyalty helps bring in revenue.

Something important to understand is that emotional weight is not always proportional to problem size. In other words, a small irritation can create a large emotional reaction, especially if it happens repeatedly. A glitchy app button that you need to tap ten times a day for it to work will build stress in you.

A 15-second process that should be instant will add more stress to an already busy schedule. These micro-moments of frustration matter because they tend to pile up.

That's the key. It's not the size of the problem; it's the frequency multiplied by friction.

Let's say someone spends three hours each day manually formatting their social media posts because their design tool doesn't support batch editing. That's three hours a day, 21 hours a week, over 1,000 hours a year. Now multiply that by 10,000 users. That's hours of wasted minutes annually, just from one small design flaw or limitation.

Now imagine that you're the one who has the skill set and the tools to fix that.

You don't just save people time, you save them *mental drag, stress, anger, and frustration.* You become the name they associate with clarity, solution, and relief. And you didn't need to invent something radical. You just needed to *notice and act on the small thing no one else took seriously.*

Here's another angle to consider: micro irritations create silent churn within people. People may not leave your product or platform in a dramatic breakup. They will slowly disengage when a small irritant exists in your system and you have overlooked it for a long time, hoping it may self-correct. They quietly start looking for alternatives. They may also recommend other sites to friends. They will eventually ghost you. And it's all because of the little annoyances that went unaddressed.

Now flip that. If you're the person who solves *those* problems, you'll attract users who feel *seen.* And when people feel seen, especially in their daily struggles, they will stick around because trust is built in the details.

To find these kinds of opportunities, you have to pay attention. Become hypersensitive to friction in your own life. When you repeat a task, ask yourself, "Can it be done more easily and refined to have a better user experience?" When you use any tool, ask yourself, "What can I do differently by adding more features to this tool?" When you see others complain, don't brush it off, zoom in and analyse.

Some of the most powerful prompts you can use may include:

- "What is it that I do every day that feels much harder than it should be?"

- "Where do I see people creating hacks, templates, or workarounds?"

- "What part of this process would I pay to never have to repeat it repeatedly?"

- "Where am I wasting time on something repetitive that requires manual input, and something that is poorly designed?"

Micro-irritations are everywhere in education, healthcare, digital marketing, remote work, parenting, fitness, and e-commerce. Whenever you have to do something manually that could be automated, that's a business idea. Whenever you have to explain the same concept to someone for the fifth time, there's room for better onboarding and communication. Whenever someone says, "I hate this part," you have a lead. It's time to bring in automation and automate the process.

The beauty of solving micro-irritations is that the barrier to entry is often lower. You don't need to revolutionize an industry. You just need to build something clean, effective, and user-friendly. Start small, solve well, and let the word of mouth carry your work to millions.

Also, when you fix smaller annoyances, you open doors to help solve much *bigger problems*. A product that starts by solving a minor frustration often grows into a platform that solves much more. It becomes the gateway drug to business. People come in for convenience but stay on for the transformation.

So don't underestimate the tiny things. They may not seem flashy or significant, but they help stack. And the ones who remove friction, no matter how small, become heroes in someone's daily routine.

A saying goes like this: *"Don't wait for the world to fall apart to offer help, look for where it's quietly breaking down."* That's your role now. You are not just an observer of the chaos but a pattern-seeker. A builder. A fixer of small things that create big relief.

The world doesn't need more big ideas.

More people are needed who pay attention to *the little ones that matter.*

Finding Opportunity in Repetition– If People Keep Doing It, It's Worth Solving

Pay attention to repetition if you want to build a business that scales. Not your own, but the repetitive behaviors of others. The tasks they repeat. The habits they repeat. The complaints they repeat. Repetition is a neon sign pointing directly at what matters in people's lives. And more importantly, what's costing them time, energy, and attention?

Here's the truth: people repeat what's necessary, not always what's efficient. They repeat what "works" well enough to get by. But just because something gets done doesn't mean it's optimized. Just because people have adapted doesn't mean they're satisfied. And just because they're doing it repeatedly doesn't mean it's the best way forward.

That's where you come in.

Every repetitive behavior, especially the ones people don't love doing, is an *invitation*. An invitation to step in and say, "What if this were easier? Faster? Smarter? Done for you?" That's not just a convenience, it's a business model.

Let's get specific. Think about how many small, tedious tasks fill someone's day: replying to similar emails, scheduling calls, entering expenses, uploading content, reformatting documents, exporting data, taking notes, proofreading, and sending reminders. These are all things people do *daily*, often without questioning them.

Why? Because they feel routine. And routine is deceptive. It disguises waste as structure.

But for the entrepreneur who's paying attention, routine is the ultimate resource. It tells you exactly where people are spending time. And time is money. This is where both time and money are being wasted right under our noses and in plain sight. Wouldn't someone question that? Most won't. But would you?

Let's consider a basic example: calendar scheduling. Before online tools and apps, people spent an absurd amount of time emailing back and forth to find a time to meet. "Are you free on Thursday at 2.00 pm?" "No, what about Friday morning?" "That doesn't work for me." On and on it went. That was standard. But it was also *painful*—and invisible. It had hidden frustration building up on both ends. But, societal formalities and mutual respect between both parties had helped keep that hidden steam pipe buried and prevented it from bursting.

Many apps that came into existence didn't bring about any new behavioral changes. It solved an old one that was a repetition of the past. And it became a frustrating one.

That's the secret: you don't need to create new habits. You need to *meet existing ones* and improve them. Meet them somewhere in the middle and make changes for today's use.

This principle works across every industry. Writers using the same editing steps? Are parents making the same repetitive weekly grocery list? I think so. The solution might be to offer a smart shopping template. Coaches sending the same onboarding emails? Help them create a white-labeled automation tool. Repetition isn't boring, it's *predictable*. And predictability makes systems, and proven systems help scale.

Even better? Repetition equals data. When people repeat something over and over, they start to create patterns. Patterns of preference, mistakes, shortcuts, and timing. All of those are valuable insights. If you solve a repeated behavior, you also start collecting behavioral data that helps you optimize, personalize, and iterate.

That's not just helpful; it's a competitive advantage.

There's another layer here: *emotional repetition*. This happens when someone keeps coming back to face the same frustration, even though the task is different. Why? Is it because there are no other available options? A business owner who's always behind on bookkeeping. A student who's constantly cramming the night before exams. A social media manager who dreads writing captions. These tasks might shift, but the *feelings* remain the same. That emotional loop tells you that there is something much more profound: this problem isn't just annoying, it's mentally draining.

When something persistently drains people's energy, they will be willing to pay to have it removed.

It might look like just a mere $19/month subscription. It might be just a one-time course. It might be an annual license. But people don't just buy products—they buy relief from *repeated stress*. That money may not mean much to them, but the relief from stress? That will be priceless to them. That $19 may feel like pocket change to them in the grand scheme. But they are willing to pay the price. If they only feel it once, they'll live with it. If they feel it all the time, they'll look for help. Your help, hopefully.

This is why recurring revenue models such as subscriptions work so well: they're built around the idea that people want *ongoing support* for ongoing problems. You're not solving a one-time event; you're solving a repeating pattern.

Let's go even deeper. Repetition also creates *skill gaps*. When someone takes on a task frequently but executes it poorly, they eventually realize: "There has to be a better way." That's when they start searching for answers. That's when they start downloading and testing. That's when they are prepared to start paying.

You're not just competing with other products. You're competing with *their habit*. If their habit is broken, inefficient, or outdated—but familiar—they'll keep doing it until someone helps make the switch easy. That's why your solution must be practical and easier than their current behavior: bad habits are sticky, and old habits die hard.

You have to offer them *a better routine*. A better outcome with less effort. A cleaner loop.

Let's look at a few ways you can turn repetition into revenue:

1. **Build Tools That Automate**: Anything repetitive can be systematized. Ask yourself, "Can I build something that does this task automatically for the user each time so they never have to touch it again for it to keep working?"

2. **Create Templates and Shortcuts**: Repetition isn't always something you can eliminate; it's something you help speed up. Think checklists, scripts, frameworks, and batch solutions.

3. **Offer Done-For-You Services**: If people keep repeating a task but hate doing it, they'll gladly pay someone else to handle it.

4. **Train People to Do It Smarter**: Training materials become the product if repetition is inevitable (like

parenting or managing a team). A course. A playbook. A strategy guide.

5. **Bundle and Monetize the Routine**: Package several small solutions into a cohesive ecosystem. Think templates, whiteboards, integration systems, and productivity kits.

Your value is in how well you understand the *real rhythm* of someone's day. What are they doing over and over again? What's the turning point at which a task turns into a chore? At what point do they sigh and say, "Here we go again"?

That's your in.

One final insight: If people are repeating something without knowing why it is being repeated, they are *ripe for disruption and will be awaiting it. Until then, they will be continuing to do what they are doing, because it is safe and comfortable for them.* They're not emotionally attached to the task; they're just doing it out of habit. When you come along with a smarter, faster, more intuitive method, switching becomes effortless.

Think of how fast people have abandoned traditional maps for GPS. Or how quickly people stopped downloading songs or buying CDs and DVDs and switched to streaming. How many other programs have replaced endless email chains with a cleaner chat workflow?

When repetition is loud but loyalty is weak, you've got leverage.

So don't chase the glamorous, complex problems just yet. Start with the obvious ones, the ones hiding in plain sight. The to-dos. The defaults. The "I've always done it this way" routines.

Because if they're repeating it, they're ready to rethink it.

And when they rethink, and if your solution is ready and waiting for them-you, you will inevitably win.

The Sweet Spot -Where Frustration, Frequency, and Urgency Overlap

In business, not every problem is created equal. Some are loud but rare. Others are frequent but tolerable. A few are urgent but low-friction. These may spark interest, but they rarely spark transactions. If you want to build something that makes money, moves fast, and matters deeply, you have to aim for what I call the sweet spot where frustration, frequency, and urgency all live in the same space and meet at a common intersection.

That intersection is where the real magic happens.

Let's define these clearly:

- **Frustration** is the emotional pain. It's the stress, the exhaustion, the silent rage people feel when things don't work the way they should.

- **Frequency** is how often the pain shows up. Daily? Weekly? Monthly or Yearly? Is it every time someone uses a tool, interacts with a system, or faces a situation?

- **Urgency** is the level of pressure the problem creates. Does it need to be fixed now, or can we wait it out?

When these three align, you're not just solving a problem-you're addressing a felt need that can't be ignored. People will pay fast, repeatedly, and gratefully for solutions that can be solved in this fast zone.

Here's why this sweet spot is so powerful: it filters out the noise and the drama.

85

Too many entrepreneurs waste energy solving problems, which is only *one* of these things. For example, something might be frustrating, but rare, such as dealing with customer service once a year. It's annoying, but not urgent or frequent enough to drive purchases. Or a task that might be frequently performed but is painless, like brushing your teeth. Sure, it happens every day, but unless there's friction, there's nothing over there to fix.

Likewise, something might feel urgent but isn't frequent, like filing taxes. It matters, but it only happens once a year. Unless you build around that seasonality (like accounting software), the opportunity is narrow.

But when you find something people do *often*, that also feels *bad*, and they want it fixed *now*, you've got a business with teeth. You can grind through anything by commanding top dollars for your unique product or service that is premium, unique, and in high demand.

Let's look at some real-world examples.

Think of the daily frustration faced by many remote teams around scheduling meetings across time zones. The problem surfaces pretty frequently (multiple times per week), causes frustration (confusion, missed meetings, wasted time), and is urgent (it has to be resolved quickly). That's why various tools that have been created to solve that fall in that intersection have gained traction. They help solve something that's not just inconvenient—it's *consistently disruptive*.

Now consider people with chronic illnesses like diabetes. They need to check their blood sugar, manage food intake, and track symptoms. That's a frequent affair to partake in daily. It can be deeply frustrating, especially when devices or data tracking aren't user-friendly. And it's urgent because poor tracking can have life-threatening consequences. That's why healthtech apps and smart monitors in this space have thrived for years, not just survived.

Frustration alone doesn't sell. Frequency alone doesn't scale. Urgency alone doesn't last. But all three together? That's a goldmine.

Here's how to start spotting these sweet spot opportunities in the wild.

Start by interviewing users or, better yet, observing them. Watch where they *visibly show a struggle*. What do they keep doing that causes a frown, a sigh, or a muttered "ugh"? Don't just take note of the action, track the context. How often does it happen? What does it cost them in terms of time, energy, and outcome? Do they *need* to do it right now, or could they wait?

You'll start noticing patterns.

Let's say you're studying content creators. You might find that writing video descriptions is a recurring task. It needs to get done several times a week (frequency), it's tedious and uncreative (frustration), and it's required to publish the content (urgency) on time. Bingo. There's a software opportunity.

Now imagine you're talking to parents who are trying to get their kids ready for school. Every morning, they face the same battle. Packing lunches. Finding shoes. Forgotten homework. It's frustrating. It happens daily. And it can't be delayed. That's a sweet spot. Maybe the solution is a night-before checklist app or an AI-based prep assistant that can help create custom routines.

You're not just solving pain. You're solving *repetitive, emotional, time-sensitive* pain.

That's the difference.

Another way to find this sweet spot is to audit your own life. Track what tasks cause you the most stress over a week. Make three columns: Frequency, Frustration, and Urgency. Then list your common tasks or struggles. This may help you zero in on your next endeavor.

You might be surprised. Something you've just "gotten used to" might actually be the seed of a scalable business.

Let's say, every day, you find yourself wasting 15 minutes formatting client documents. It's not thrilling work. It adds no real value to your day-to-day affairs. But it has to be done, and it annoys you every single time. You've just identified a sweet spot.

Now, the next step is to validate that others feel the same as you. If you're annoyed and they're annoyed, and it's happening at scale, *you've got something real.*

Here's a key insight: businesses built in the sweet spot tend to grow faster. Why? Because the need is obvious, the payoff is immediate, and the solution spreads by word of mouth. People love to share solutions that have *saved them from pain.* It makes them feel like heroes. That's how you create natural referrals.

To top it off, sweet spot problems create loyalty. If you relieve the pressure people feel *every day*, they won't easily switch to a competitor. They're emotionally invested in what you've built. You have now become part of their routine. Their relief becomes your retention.

You also get to uphold your *pricing power.* When urgency is high, people aren't price shopping—they're pain shopping. They want the thing that helps give them relief now. This means you can charge them a premium for convenience, speed, and simplicity.

But with great opportunity comes one warning: don't overcomplicate the solution by keeping it simple, clear, and easy to use.

The very thing that makes a sweet spot problem powerful—its simplicity. This can be destroyed if your offer is bloated, confusing, or overbuilt. The goal is to reduce friction, not replace it with a different, hard-to-use solution.

So, build something focused. Elegant. Human-centered. Let the relief speak for itself.

To recap:

- The best problems to solve are the ones that are *frequent*, *frustrating*, and *urgent*.

- These problems create the highest willingness to pay, inviting customers to refer, and the ability of the customer to stay loyal to your brand.

- You can spot them by observing their behavior, listening for emotional energy, and auditing them from your own experience.

- Simplicity always wins. Build for clarity and ease, not complexity and hype.

If you can find one sweet spot problem and build one clean solution, you've already won more than most can offer in a product or service.

Because in a world full of people chasing attention, you'll be the one who's actually solving something that *hurts*.

And that's where the real wealth begins.

CHAPTER 4

Tools for Problem Discovery

"You can't solve a problem that you don't fully understand. And you can't understand it unless you listen to it deeply or live it yourself." You will need to live it, to experience it, and understand its inner workings.

The goldmine of any business idea is buried in conversations. Conversations not only with oneself or one's mind, but with the environment, the people around us, the community we live in, and the world at large. It's not in your head. It's in the language of your market.

Imagine sitting with a customer on the verge of tears because of a tiny problem that ruined her entire day. A simple problem that could be solved and has the potential to become a goldmine if only one could find a possible solution to solve this problem. It doesn't have to solve the world's problems, but just this particular one that people face daily.

The things we have today were a result of problems that arose in the past, and the solutions were a result of people's ideas. Anything you see around you is someone's idea. Solutions don't sprout overnight. Each solution started its journey from complaints; from these complaints, the budding ideas came into being, and these ideas led to business creation.

There are several ways by which anyone can help solve problems. The first step is to understand the problems and needs of others. Once you give people what they need and what they are seeking, the money will follow automatically. If your product or service is much better than your competitor's and you relieve them, you do not need to say a word. Your products and services will speak for themselves.

What am I arriving at, you may ask? There are many ways to look for problems when one gets stuck and does not know how to find them. Here are a few notable ones:

1. Surveys

This involves conversing with people directly, paying attention to what they are saying and what they aren't, their words, actions, and body language. Oftentimes, non-verbal communication gives us more information than verbal conversations do. To identify a problem, one must read between the lines. Not all information that is valuable is said; sometimes it is felt.

Surveys are not all about Q&A sessions; they are emotional excavations. They help to understand the root cause of frustrations, unmet needs, and deep-seated desires. They go far beyond the surface level; they dig deeper into the complaints of the general public, which in turn helps to identify potential problems they may have, which we can help solve.

While trying to identify problems to solve, it is important to note that there are problems out there waiting to be solved by us. Since we were never taught to zero in on others' problems, we have become ignorant of the subject and have stayed in the darkness too long. Some may already have their solutions embedded in them, and they may be waiting for the right person to take note, take the initiative, and put them into action to yield tangible results.

These interviews are about listening closely, not selling, coaching, or explaining, but about listening, understanding, and being able to relate to potential customers and their problems at a level that makes them feel heard and comfortable to voice their opinion. Even without having a product to help solve their problems straight away, they have already felt a sense of comfort and understanding by having been "felt" and "listened to" by the surveyors.

By asking open-ended questions, let the people tell you what they want, expect in terms of relief, and what they want the outcome to be. Open-ended questions may present themselves as:

- "What's the hardest part of your day?"
- "What do you wish to get fixed?"
- "Have you tried to solve this before?"
- "What went wrong?"
- "What is your expectation this time around?"
- "How fast do you want it to get solved?"
- "Would you be able to do what it takes to help you recover?"
- "What is the intensity, duration, urgency, and severity of your problems?"

Capture the words, their tone of voice, and emotional spikes. How they react to certain questions when asked. Every subtle change should be noted to effectively and efficiently fix the problem. Record every interview if need be.

Ensure to read them later and look for patterns. These serve as guides and treasure maps required to identify the problem. By connecting the dots, we could create a pattern from which a solution to the problem can be formulated.

2. Forums

Now, think of platforms that contain endless streams of raw, unfiltered data, a treasure trove of complaints, confusion, daily struggles, annoyances, regrets about wasted time, efforts, and loss of money, etc. As with social media usage, spikes in usage lead people to be more likely to say things openly on these platforms than they would in real life.

Without even being asked, people are ready to vent and rant about their daily personal struggles on public platforms. This suggests that people are publicly seeking help, waiting for someone to assist them in solving their problems and innovating to reform existing products that have become obsolete, thereby bringing them to life and potentially helping them.

But how does one utilize these digital confession booths to suit and create solutions for what one may be looking for? These platforms showcase an endless abyss of problems. The commonality of all of them is that they are waiting for answers and are actively seeking relief.

You can't solve the world's problems in one go. It cannot be done. But you can pick just a small fraction of it and focus on that portion of the much larger pie.

Pick a niche, develop on it, nurture it, be consistent, and be disciplined to watch it grow. What started as a simple way to help one person with one problem, you might end up saving humanity.

How does one filter out such information? We do this by using keyword searches, like:

- "I hate when..."
- "Trying to..."
- "Can someone tell me why…?"

93

- "Why does it always..."

- "Can someone please help me with..."

These, among others, can be used to get specific information off the internet. Public cries for help like these are from people pointing out their problems indirectly and waiting for a hero to solve their problems. Multiple market signals send distress calls out to anyone willing to lend an ear and a helping hand.

3. Casual Conversations

You never know where your next inspiration might come from. It might come from a brief interaction with a driver on the way home, or from the delivery guy at the door, a Slack rant from a coworker, a random conversation at the family dinner table, etc.

The sad part is, people don't listen to the world around them. Every day, conversations are filled with both noise and opportunities. We only want to listen to what we want and not pay attention to anything else. We have also stopped listening intently due to the many distractions and noise around us.

To tap into the right frequency, you must understand that you are not socializing but in detecting mode. Detecting and identifying problems and finding their root causes can help solve them. It's not hard to detect such expressions that stand for real-life problems, but to detect and zero in, one must fine-tune one's mind towards them. For example:

- "This takes too long..."

- "I wish there was an easier way..."

- "It's so annoying when..."

Train your mind to perk up and listen to such words that signify the problems they are facing. Pick a pen, and write down on paper. If one person is saying it, thousands are thinking it. You can fix that just by listening and acting on those. It may put on someone's face, all because you listened keenly and acted on it to bring them a solution.

They may be difficult at first, but will be rewarding in the end.

4. Brainstorming Sessions

You don't need to know it all or have a well-defined or finite idea right now, and you might not have all the answers, but that will be the start of your journey. Sometimes, all you need is a whiteboard, a marker, five curious people, and a killer, ground-breaking question:

"What problems do people deal with daily that we can help solve?"

This question alone can raise a thousand answers. Why? Because of the curious, creative minds of individuals. It may take some rumination among brilliant minds to set yourself on the right track.

Bringing together the curiosity and intelligence of several people deliberating on a particular issue reveals new paths one cannot even begin to fathom. There are many paths to a common goal. Each person brings something to the table; the magic happens when that concoction is done.

Brainstorming sessions are spontaneous and unpredictable, so editing at this stage is not advised. Let the ideas float and watch how many different pathways form. The best ideas often sound ridiculous initially, but when one moves and flows with the chaos, things tend to take shape based on inner vision.

Even bad ideas sometimes have good endings. You can always refine it later. But for now, hold on to the chaos and the idea and see where it leads. It's like a painter having an idea in their mind to paint. They start with their initial vision and specifications for the painting. But as the work progresses, the scenery and the vision change. It may or may not take them into an entirely different realm. It may or may not shift from their initially envisioned picture. The painting will show its true colors, transforming with each brush stroke and paint dip.

A creative mindset has endless ideas and thought processes; multiply that mind by Five X or Ten X and place them in a single room with a whiteboard. Then, watch how the magic unfolds to take on different forms around them.

5. Client and Team Meetings

If you are already working with clients, you have a never-ending front-row seat to problems you must deal with regularly. You must ask the right questions to fully understand what is required and how to tackle it most professionally and efficiently. Your clients will most likely know firsthand what they need, and sometimes may not. It's now up to you to decide what's being said and expected of you, then develop on it by understanding it in depth, before putting it into action.

The same is to be conveyed to the team. The lack of understanding and miscommunication may have shortened the lives of many failed projects. Listen to people and get feedback from those who manage logistics, answer emails, and interact with customers daily. Since they see their problems up close and personal and live them and breathe them, they would be the best people to bring them on board. Sometimes, the breakthrough isn't by solving old problems, but by solving existing ones through modification and transformation.

Get your team on board, lay out the blueprint, and make sure everyone is on the same page. Then bring out the goal for the week, the month, and the year. Hold people accountable for their respective tasks and maximize their skills to accomplish what needs to be done within the specific period. When work gets done in an organized fashion, stress and chaos take the back seat. Results come into focus with productivity and profits on the balance sheets.

THE HAVES AND THE HAVE-NOTS

CHAPTER 5

Focus and Validate

"The enemy of success isn't failure. It's distraction."
You may have discovered dozens of problems by now. Many exciting things you want to dabble in and get involved with. But when one gets exposed to so many problems, questions will emerge:

- "How do you know which one to focus on?"
- "Which can one build around an existing product or service?"
- "Which one would benefit not only me but everyone else?"
- "How do I actualize the solutions to solve the ideas?"
- "Which one has the most incentive for making *money*?"

This chapter will help you narrow down and validate before you build anything.

In the early stages of building a business or solving a problem, it's tempting to chase every idea that comes to mind. You want to become a jack of all trades by extending your tentacles like an octopus and focusing on ten problems simultaneously, trying to serve everyone worldwide. As alluring as it sounds, one might get more than they bargained for.

Here's the brutal truth,

"If you're solving everything at once, you're solving nothing."

Let that sink in well; I read it multiple times. It's easy to get carried away with everything. We may even start losing our focus and watching our neighbors to see what they are doing and to see what they are succeeding at. We will lose our focus, lane, and goal in that process.

Success doesn't come from scattering your energy and resources across a dozen problems, trying to do everything and solve everything. It comes from owning one problem so deeply, unapologetically, that your solution becomes the go-to for everyone.

Eventually and in due course, you will build a name for yourself around your brand and become the sought-after guy or gal for your specialized skill. That's the beauty of staying in your lane and not losing focus, no matter how long it takes.

"Great businesses start by going narrow and deep, not wide and shallow."

Only after you have focused on one skill or path for many years will you be able to master it. Only at that stage should you finally diversify. At that time, your accessory pipelines will complement your primary ones. They will feed on each other and can help bring in revenue by creating multiple income streams. This is what the wealthy do. They focus on one thing for a very long time. Once they reach the top in their chosen industry, they acquire businesses that complement their original revenue stream, eventually buying out competitors and smaller companies to scale exponentially.

You may have heard the saying like this: "Jack of all trades, Master of none."

BECOME THE MASTER OF ONE BUSINESS: *Choose One Problem or Service and Own It.*

In business, *timing matters*. Early on, you don't have the luxury of being broad. You needed to focus. Choose one pain point. Validate it. Own it. Make people say:

"This is exactly what I've been looking for."

In the early days of building a solution, whether a product, a service, or a life-changing app, there's a captivating trap many people fall into. I cannot emphasize this enough: *trying to solve everything*. With too many problems around, we will tend to lose focus.

You come across one problem and think, *"I can fix this."* Then you see another. *"This, too."* Before long, you're juggling ten problems, wearing ten hats, and telling yourself you're being productive. You are essentially tricking yourself by being busy. You are spinning your wheels, but are you moving? You're diluting your impact and brewing chaos before putting yourself out there.

The phrase that I mentioned earlier:

"Jack of all trades, Master of none."

It's often a warning: don't spread yourself too thin, or you'll be mediocre at everything. You may also lose focus.

Master one first, then expand later on when the timing is right. Having multiple skills is good, but the train will come off the rails without focus.

That line speaks to the power of having multiple skill sets and being able to adapt and build across domains. It's a strength to be used only at the right stage. Again, Timing.

At the validation stage, versatility is not the goal. Precision is.

You need to choose one problem and go deep. Own it like your life depends on it. Learn its pains, its patterns, and the people affected by it. You can't validate ten ideas at once. But you can validate one, so deeply and thoroughly. If you want to make a lasting and meaningful impact, you need to focus on one, not many. And that one validated idea might become the cornerstone of your empire.

Will People Pay for This Solution? Practical Validation Methods

Now comes the real test: proof that the problem is real, that the solution solves the problem, and that people would be willing to pay for the solution. This alone separates wishful thinking from market-ready brilliance. The goal of validation is not to seek perfection but to gather proof.

So, focus, test, learn, iterate. Then you can build through confidence and not by guesswork. You'd have a well-thought-out plan to execute, so people will want to pay for the product they desire.

It's not enough when people say,

- "Oh, that's a brilliant idea"
- "This could work well"
- "I love your concept."

These might be just superficial conversations. People may say it to please you and out of obligation. But you want to hear the truth, not a sugarcoated lie.

You need the product to speak for them and to you authentically, and to speak volumes; the product needs them to say:

- "Take my money"
- "Is it market-ready? I want to buy it now."
- "Can I help test it?"

- "I'm telling all my family and friends about it."

When this happens, you will have social proof of concept.

Real Validation is Transactional

Validation doesn't come from compliments, likes, or vague interests. It comes when someone pays, signs up, commits, or wants to invest in whatever you are building. You will need to tell them it's valuable, and they need to know within themselves. Until then, it's just noise.

The harsh truth is,

"If people won't pay you for it, it's not a business, it's a hobby."

Practical Validation Methods

Here are some Practical Validation Methods to test if people will *pay* for your solution:

1. Pre-Sell Your Product

Before building the full version, consider a prototype, propose an offer, be pre-order ready, offer early access, or stock a discounted beta version of the product.

Ask yourself, "If I built this product, would people pay $X?" If they are hesitant or skeptical about it, dig deeper; You may find that there are key features you are missing out or lacking in adequate development. If no one's buying, take the hint: it's either the wrong solution to the problem, focusing on the wrong problem, it's the wrong pitch, or you are focusing on the wrong audience. But instead, if they imply "Take my money", you've struck gold.

2. Run a Fake-Feature Test

If you're building a unique product, test the demand for a portion of your product line that is similar, before embarking on building the whole product. Otherwise, you might end up manufacturing a product no one would be interested in or wouldn't pay for. Test by offering the features as if they already exist. You are testing the market interest here. Start by tracking clicks, interests, and tone in voice. You're not lying, you're validating. You're building the change people want to see based on their demands. You're helping them by making enquiries as you focus on building by feeling the vibe of market conditions.

Don't hide behind your ideas and products. Showcase them because they are your babies; don't expect them to succeed overnight. Look beyond your ego; this isn't about you, it's about you solving a problem by taking action towards it. Talk to the target audience, the real buyers, the real critics, and the actual users of your product

- "What would make this a no-brainer?"
- "What do you hate about existing solutions?"
- "If this worked perfectly, how would your life change?"

You're not just validating a product. You're validating *urgency*. It is this urgency that the audience is waiting for to be satisfied. The more people say, "I need this now," the more viable your product or service idea.

3. Pilot Programs and Paid Trials

Launch an MVP, a small, private version of your service or product. To further the project, you may charge a modest fee or make it free. This will make people curious enough to test the product or service. If people start signing up, even with the starter flaws and limitations, you've hit a real breakthrough and are on the right track. Now, all that's left is to build from there, developing and tweaking continuously, not forgetting to follow up with enquiries and questions from beta testers.

Authentic feedback from genuine users is 10x more valuable than straight and assumed guesses. Most importantly, you will know your target audiences only by asking the right questions and getting uncomfortable answers.

This is how you will learn, adapt, and grow. Growth happens outside your comfort zone. So, get comfortable being uncomfortable. Once that happens, you will go all in. Most people are comfortable following others and hence do not want to venture far from their home turf. That is a self-limiting behavior that limits growth, knowledge, innovation, and open-mindedness. Following the herd is much easier than carving out your own path. Thus, many become followers.

DESIGNING SOLUTIONS THAT WILL SELL

CHAPTER 6

Understand the Root Cause

In business and life, too many solutions are fabricated to work for the time being and are considered temporary fixes. Quick patches. Surface-level fixes. They soothe the pain temporarily until you find a better solution, but they don't stop it from returning.

That's because most people treat symptoms, not the root causes. And that's the trap.

If every manufactured medicine cured all illnesses permanently, those companies would be instantly out of business. Think about it. The medicine we see all around us may be designed to mask the symptoms and help you get through the day with minimal suffering.

But what about a permanent cure? That may not exist in an ideal world. For example, if someone had found a permanent cure for the common cold, all the pharmacy shelves would be empty. Who would visit the doctor?

Now picture an iceberg. What you see above the water line is the complaints we hear about: "We are not hitting the sales target set for this week," "Sales are dropping," "Our teams are not communicating well with each other." But the real reason, the root cause dragging the entire situation down to the core, is probably hidden miles beneath the surface.

If you don't dig deeper, you'll build solutions for the wrong problems.

A restaurant owner might complain:

"Customers just don't come back. Maybe we need better ads."

So they start pouring money into marketing. More ads. More discounts. More influencer hype. And for a while, traffic may increase.

But then it drops again.

Someone finally walks in and asks, "Why don't you guys use air conditioners? It's always hot in here."

The problem wasn't visibility, it was comfort. This was the root cause that had caused a ripple effect to the detriment of the food establishment.

They were trying to solve a visibility problem when, in fact, they had a comfort level problem.
Root cause? Poor in-store experience. Long lines. Low returning customers.

Rule #1: Ask "Why?" Until It Hurts

There's a concept from a lean manufacturing company called the **"5 Whys."** The rule is: To get to the root of any problem, ask "Why?" List at least five relevant questions that apply to the situation.

Problem: The project is always late.

1. Why? Because tasks aren't finished on time.

2. Why? Because people miss deadlines.

3. Why? Because they're unclear on priorities.

4. Why? Because we didn't assign clear deadlines.

5. Why? Because we never set them in the first place.

Root cause: **No priority-setting system.** That's what you need to fix.

The Pain Beneath the Pain

Here's something else no one tells you about: most problems are not what people say they are. These answers are never straightforward, but twisted. You will need to dig into them to get the right answers.

"I hate budgeting."

They don't. They hate the guilt of seeing where their money went, and now they are upset. They are channeling their frustrations away from their source.

"My team never communicates." Maybe they do. But they don't feel safe being honest, and maybe it's because no one is willing to listen.

"I need more sales." Sometimes, they don't. They need better retention so fewer people leave. This may be a lack of satisfaction with a product or service.

To solve what people truly need, you must deep dive into the emotions behind the issue.

Guilt.

Fear.

Insecurity.

Uncertainty.

Shame.

That's where the root pain usually lives.

A Founder's Trap: Solving What Feels Comfortable

Many first-time founders love solving problems that make them feel smart—but not the ones that make them feel uncomfortable. They'd rather build a dashboard than pick up the phone to ask a customer what went wrong. It may also be an ego issue.

Comfort is a dangerous compass.

If you only fix what feels familiar, you'll miss the cracks underneath your business.

Why Do We Avoid Root Causes?

Most people don't avoid root causes because they're lazy. They avoid them because they're emotional.

Here's why:

- Root causes often point to you, not the product, service, the employee, or the market. It's you.

- Root causes force you to face your fears, flaws, and habits. Which you are uncomfortable facing. You also do not want to face reality.

- Root causes require humility before they give you leverage.

Let that sink in.

The more personal a problem feels, the more likely it is the right one to solve. The deeper the discomfort, the higher the return.

How to Find the Root Cause?

Here's a simple method to uncover root causes without second-guessing:

1. Observe First, Solve Later
Before offering a solution, watch how people behave in their natural environment. Not in surveys. Not in a room. In the wild, the animals roam free and aren't aware they are being

watched. This is the natural way to take a peek at the causative factors.

What do they avoid? Where do they freeze? What's their facial expression like when they do this task?

2. Ask: What Would You do if we could make this Problem Disappear?

This is key. If removing the problem doesn't change much, it's not the root cause.

But if removing it causes **everything else to shift**, it's bingo. You have nailed it in the head.

3. Separate Cause from Coincidence

Just because two things happen together doesn't mean one caused the other.

Sales had been dropping since our website was redesigned. Maybe. But maybe the season or customer interests have changed.

Always verify before you act.

Patterns of Root Problems in Different Industries

Let's break this down into verticals so you can begin spotting them wherever you work:

In Tech:
- Symptom: "The product isn't scaling."
- Root Cause: You built for early adopters, not the mainstream user. The UX is too complex and not user-friendly.

In Healthcare:
- Symptom: "Patients don't follow their medication schedule."

- Root Cause: The instructions are confusing, and the cost of the medicine forces them to skip doses or stop them altogether to save money. Maybe they forget because the solution isn't tied into their routine.

In Education:

- Symptom: "Students aren't learning and are not hitting the top grades".

- Root Cause: The system rewards memorization, not understanding. Maybe, the learning environment is fear-based instead of curiosity-driven.

In Relationships:

- Symptom: "We keep arguing over the same things."

- Root Cause: You're not arguing because of the problem. You are arguing about not being heard or being respected at home.

The solution isn't always to look for a new tool.

Sometimes, it's to discover a new truth. The real truth, and then get going from there.

Building from the Bottom, Not from the Top

Once you've uncovered the root cause, don't rush to wrap it in features, packaging, or marketing.

Take a step back and ask:

"If I could solve this at its absolute root cause…

What would the most elegant, invisible solution look like?"

Remember:

- True value doesn't always shout. It whispers into your user's ears daily.

- The best solutions feel inevitable once seen.

- The user says, "How did I ever live without this?"

Take note-taking apps, for example. The root problem it had wasn't about note-taking at all, but it was about fragmented thinking. People were managing ideas, projects, and databases using five different tools.

So they got to work with the core concept, "Let's build one clean canvas that adapts to your brain, and give it one place to put all things together for ease and comfort."

Hence, they created a solution for cognitive flow, and not just for information storage.

Root cause: scattered systems.

Solution: Integration and unification of multiple applications into one.

The 3 Filters Before You Build

To summarize, run every idea through these three filters before building anything:

1. **Is this the root cause, or does it categorize as a symptom?**

2. If it's a symptom, dig deeper. If it's the cause, stay here and work at it.

3. **If I fix this one thing, what else will improve automatically?**

4. Look for domino effects. That's where leverage lives.

5. **Would the user say: 'This solved something I didn't know I needed'**

6. That's root-level transformation. That's the stuff of sticky products, viral referrals, and premium pricing.

The Root is Where the Money Hides

Most people don't want to dig in. That's where you come in to tap into your advantageous side.

You're not here to slap stickers on broken pipes.

You're here to stop the leak once and for all.

Because when you solve the right problem,

You don't need to shout about it.

The relief will speak for you and on your behalf. All you have to do is to stay silent, observe, and look for the next big problem to solve.

THE WEALTH INEQUALITY

CHAPTER 7

From Insight to Innovation

Now that you have dissected root causes, how do we turn this insight into Innovation? Innovation is not magic. It's not lightning in a bottle.

It's pattern recognition. It's empathy. It's the discipline and the art of listening, for the solution starts whispering.

Many innovators and inventors jump from idea to idea without having the patience to sit on it. They become impatient to wait and see the outcome. They want to move on and solve world problems.

They move fast but shallow. They confuse novelty with usefulness. They think invention is innovation. It's not.

Invention is creating something new and novel in the world. Innovation is creating something *better*.

And better only matters if it makes someone's life *easier*, *faster*, *cheaper*, and *more meaningful*.

Innovation Starts with a Sharp Insight

An insight is not just an observation. It's not what the user said, but what you envisioned by looking deeper. It's what they meant but couldn't articulate. And this is where you come in and help close the gap by bridging ideas.

Insight lives beneath the complaint.

Beneath the wish.

Beneath the "I wish this were easier."

Beneath the silence.

Let's break this down.

Who would pay $50 for a pair of socks? That is the question top founders would ask themselves.

Common socks are boring pieces of clothing. Cheap. Gets lost in laundry. They are given away to patients in hospitals, airplane travellers, and the homeless. No one ever cared about socks. But someone may be betting on bringing in high-quality socks to the market at a premium price. This may be happening as we speak.

That is insight.

Socks provide warmth and protection. And they do not stand out in fashion shows. They are just socks that can be mismatched, too, for the sake of fashion.

Now, let's talk about innovation.

Innovation isn't a new product; it is a new meaning attached to a common product.

That's insight at work.

Where Insights Hide?

To build something innovative, you must train yourself to listen with more than your ears and look outside the box.

Insights often hide in:

- **Repeated complaints:** "I hate doing this, not because I want to, but I have to."

- **Workarounds**: When people are building their own solutions to various problems.

- **Avoidance behavior** — when people don't do something they *should,* there's gold there. They are trying to avoid that uncomfortable situation again.

- **Time logs**: wherever people waste time, they crave better tools to avoid wasting time or to manage it.

Look for friction, hacks, avoidance, and frustration.

They're not obstacles, they're open invitations.

Innovation Frameworks: Choose Your Weapon

Once you've found a clear insight, now what? How do you **design from it**?

Here are three reliable frameworks to turn insights into innovative products and services:

1. Design Thinking

This is about empathy and iteration.

Step 1: Empathize – Talk. Listen. Observe. Keep asking *"why"* until the truth gets awkward.

Step 2: Define – State the core problem. Strip away the noise.

Step 3: Ideate – Brainstorm fast, without filter. Wild ideas welcome.

Step 4: Prototype – Build the smallest version that proves the idea.

Step 5: Test – Not for praise. But for truth.

This method keeps you grounded in the user, not your ego.

2. First Principles Thinking

Instead of copying what others are doing, break the problem down to its raw components.

Let's say you want to manufacture affordable solar panels.

Instead of saying, "Panels are expensive," and shrugging it off, start asking with inquisitiveness and curiosity:

- What are panels made of?

- Why are those materials used instead of others?

- Can they be sourced differently?

- What else can conduct and convert electricity from sunlight capture?

You refer to the laws of physics to find your answers. You will not follow industry-set norms, but create your own by filling in the blank canvas with your ideas. and not follow the industry norm.

This helps bring the cost of manufacturing and sourcing down to pennies. This will make it more affordable for the masses and for mass production. That's when your product will be the norm and the goal standard people will look up to.

3. Jobs-to-Get-Done (JTGD)
Every product is secretly hired to do a job in someone's life.

Nobody wants to use a drill. They want a hole to hang a shelf that holds their memories. This means people like to see the outcome and do not care about how it gets done. They look for the benefits it will offer them and only look for the final results.

You're not selling features.

You're solving an emotional task.

Your job is to find out what the user wants:

- What's the user trying to do?

- For what emotional or practical use are they hiring your product for?

- What are they upset about because it is not working for them?

The Trap of Optimization Over Innovation

Many entrepreneurs fall into this trap:

"Let's improve what exists." But you don't get paid more for optimization. You get paid more for transformation. There's a massive difference between breeding a faster horse and manufacturing a car. Optimization matters but only after initial innovation.

If you're solving the solution for the right root cause of the problem, you should ask yourself:

"What would this look like if it didn't exist yet?". Then build *that*. This is what people may be looking forward to.

Insight vs. Idea

Here's how to know you've struck a real insight—not just a passing idea:

Idea	Insight
"Let's build a finance app."	"People feel ashamed of checking their bank balances."
"Let's build a task manager."	"People don't want to finish their to-do lists because they overcommit."
"Let's create an AI tool."	"Employees copy-paste the same email 30 times daily and hate it."

Ideas are vague, but Insights are sharp and they hurt.

And that pain is where your innovation lives.

121

The World Doesn't Need More Stuff, It Needs More Sense

We don't need more tools.

We need tools that care.

That helps understand. And that reduces friction. That makes people feel powerful again.

If you can take one raw truth from someone's day-to-day life and build a solution that makes them sigh with relief, you've done more than innovate. You've helped heal.

And healing is the most valuable product you'll ever sell.

So don't just create.

Interpret. Translate. Transform.

Innovation isn't the future.

It's just insight, well-loved.

Most People See the Problem. Few People Sit With It to find a Solution for it.

We live in a world obsessed with speed.

Everyone wants to be first. To launch fast. To go viral.

But the best innovators don't just move fast.

They sit with the problem longer than anyone else.

They resist the urge to patch.

They *feel* the problem.

They *are immersed* in the discomfort.

They let the insight breathe until it becomes undeniable.

Most companies weren't built in a brainstorming session. The initial sketch is usually drawn on a paper napkin in a restaurant or a subway. Ideas may even come to you at midnight between 1.00 am and 4.00 am, usually during your REM sleep period. So, it's wise and prudent to have a small notebook and a pen on your nightstand by your bedside.

They were built out of frustration with facing discomfort and unease. When you are waiting in the frigid darkness and unable to find the right warm clothing, you will devise an idea to bring about a solution. By chance, this may be what most people are struggling with and are seeking solutions for. When you think and act on: *"There has to be a better way."* You will find your path. If you do not find your path, you will create one to follow.

And they will not stop there.

They will break barriers and bring about change in society.

Through transformation, they will redefine how cities live and breathe.

Big innovation may feel like small magic. But it's forged in deep patience.

When You Feel the "Aha" rush within Your Body, that's when the real insight kicks in.

It will not make sense, but it will click in your gut. You will feel it behind your eyes. It's that golden moment when you will stop talking and go silent because you've seen something true that connects with your inner self.

"People usually do not know what they want until you show it to them." Once they use your product or service, "They will *feel* it and know whether it's right for them."

The job of an innovator is to sense what others ignore.

To name what others leave unnamed.

To package clarity inside a world full of noise.

Invisible Innovation: Why the Best Tools "Disappear"?

Have you ever used a product and given it a second thought about how, where, and why it was made?

You would have commented: "I didn't even notice I was using it, but now I can't live without it." It has helped me simplify my life.

That's invisible innovation.

It works so well that it has become part of your flow. It was not a disruption. Not an app you can"launch." It has now become a part of your thinking.

Take search engines, for example.

There were:

No tutorials.

No walkthroughs.

No pitch decks.

You just typed, and then your answers appeared from out of nowhere.

The genius wasn't in the algorithm. It was in making **one box** that said:

"Just Ask."

That's insight-driven innovation:

That has made the users feel smarter, faster, and more powerful with *less effort*.

It's not about having more buttons or apps.

It's about having less friction.

Building Something New for the Second Brain

Today, people are overwhelmed. Too many tabs. Too many apps. Too much noise.

They're not looking for another tool.

They're looking for a second brain to help simplify. A trusted sidekick. Something that:

- Thinks for them before they forget
- Sorts out before they are drawn
- Reminds them without nagging
- Helps them do the right thing at the right time without overthinking

People are looking for something to offload their mental clutter.

They not only want a solution, but something that will *think* alongside you.

If you want to innovate today, don't ask: "What can I build?"

Ask: "What would my users pay me to help them *remember*, *organize*, and *automate* tasks, thereby simplifying their lives?"

What does Innovation *Feel* Like to the Users?

When you've built something truly innovative, the user often reacts in various ways:

1. **Relief**: "Finally, someone got it. What a relief".

2. **Surprise:** "I didn't know this was possible. How did he pull it off?"

3. **Loyalty**: "I'm never going back to the old ways."

4. **Addicted**: "You *have* to try this one or you may miss out."

125

5. **Quiet Dependence**: "This has just become part of how I live, and I cannot live without it."

You want them to feel like your product is something similar to the *oxygen you breathe*.

It is Not flashy. Not loud.

But Necessary. That's what insight-based innovation gives you. They provide you with not just customers but believers, who believe in you and in your products.

The Personal Story of a Woman Who Built a 7-Figure Business with just One Insight.

A working mom, juggling three kids, having a full-time job, and a side hustle. That will keep her busy. Every night, she'd lose an hour deciding what to cook. Just *deciding*.

She wasn't alone. She discovered that thousands of women were stuck in the same emotional loop: "I want to feed my family with a healthy meal, but I'm too tired to think right now."

So she built a simple app that brought all aspects of cooking and recipes together in one:

- Weekly meal plans
- Grocery lists auto-generated
- Recipes optimized for picky eaters
- Optional healthy swaps
- Meal prep steps by night-before and on the day-of

That app had made over $2M in two years.

Her innovation wasn't a recipe app. It was a decision-removal system.

She didn't sell food.

She sold mental peace, planning, and convenience.

That's what innovation rooted in empathy looks like. Not louder tech but Deeper care.

Questions to Sharpen Your Insights

Ask yourself:

- What decision are people afraid to make on their own?

- What part of their day feels like a chore?

- What outcome do they want and care about, *but procrastinate on*?

- What's the emotion behind their inaction- guilt, fear, or confusion?

- What are they already trying to solve and want solved so badly?

If you listen well enough, they'll tell you exactly what they want and what they want you to build.

Not in their words.

But in their pain, you will see it coming.

And when you respond with empathy, not ego, you'll build something unforgettable for them, which they will take to heart. Then they will go and tell others, so the word will spread.

This is how one starts from the bottom and shoots to the top.

They take themselves from being a nobody to being somebody someday. And that day will soon arrive when you know what others want and you are ready to offer them your solutions to their problems.

CHAPTER 8

Build Fast, Test Smart

"The longer your idea stays untested, the more expensive your assumptions will become."

If you're still perfecting every little feature, waiting for the right moment, or endlessly tweaking your offer behind the scenes, you're losing the very thing that gives your idea its power: **momentum**.

The moment you start building, you accelerate your path to success. When you hold back on that big dream, you delay its reality.

Perfection does not exist, and chasing something that does not exist will be a moving target that you can never achieve. Instead, work towards launching it "close to your perfection", then tweak it by creating a 2.0. Once you have it in the market, you will learn the flaws, the features that need improvement, and the ones customers seek. The market will tell you, and your customers will speak out. Thus, you will get to know them and your products. You will also learn what they like, what they dislike, and what they want in your products. This is how you will learn and grow.

You've found a significant problem. You've uncovered its root cause. Now it's time to build something that solves it—fast. But here's the truth: you don't need a perfect solution from the start.

Perfection is the enemy of progress. You need something that works, the one you can test, tweak, and improve. You must move fast, test smart, and prove your idea works before going all-in. Test fast, fail fast, and pivot as needed.

This chapter is about building something that is lean and shy: a Minimum Viable Product (MVP) that solves pain and gets people reaching for their wallets. Think of it like tossing a life raft to that drowning person in the river. It doesn't need to be a yacht; it just needs to keep them afloat until the rescue team arrives.

The Magic of the MVP

An MVP isn't a sloppy prototype or a cheap imitation. It's the *simplest version of your solution that delivers real value*. It's the first rung on the ladder, not the whole staircase.

The goal? Get it out into the world, see if it works, observe its impact, and learn how to improve it.

Imagine a young parent struggling to get their kid to sleep. Their pain is sleepless nights, stressful mornings, cranky days, and a fraying marriage. Your solution? A bedtime routine app. You don't need to build a full-on parenting platform with AI sleep tracking and lullaby playlists. You must start with a simple app that guides parents through a 10-minute bedtime ritual. That's your MVP. Quick to build, easy to test, and directly addresses the pain.

The beauty of an MVP lies in its *speed*. You're not investing years perfecting code or spending a fortune on inventory. You're building just enough to see if people will pay.

Picture a college student who noticed his classmates struggling to find affordable textbooks. His major challenge? Spending $500 a semester on books they'd use once. So what's the solution to the problem many students face today?

His MVP? A website listing free or discounted digital textbooks from legal sources. He didn't need a fancy app, a warehouse, or a massive logistical operation, but he can pull it off with just a simple website and a few hours of research. In two months, he had 300 users paying $5 a month for *access*. Not bad for a starter. That's the power of starting small and solving big.

The Feedback Goldmine

Every "no," every ignored message, every bounce from your landing page? All of these are problems for which someone is seeking solutions.

It's not considered failure. It's authentic feedback from consumers. That is data that is real. With this data in hand, you will learn:

- What language resonates with customers?"

- What solution sounds "close, but not quite there?"

- Where do people hesitate to click, and where do they rush to pay?

That's your compass. Your invisible co-founder.

A woman once launched an app to help teams collaborate remotely. She spent six months coding it herself, then a user told her they loved the service but hated the platform. Since then, she had revamped the site and made millions.

Today, building an app alone won't cut it. It must be tested thoroughly, market-ready, and must showcase impressive results.

Lesson: Build light. Test early. Iterate constantly.

The Speed Principle

Speed builds something that polish never can.

And momentum doesn't just attract customers. It attracts clarity. Focus. Feedback. Collaboration. Support.

Think of a child learning to ride a bicycle. They'll never move an inch if they wait until they understand everything about balance, wind resistance, and tire pressure. They don't need to understand its physics, but they need to act.

And if they hop on, wobble forward, and try again tomorrow, they'll figure it out *while moving.*

That's how you build smart by building forward with momentum.

The Real Goal of an MVP

An MVP is not about creating your dream solution. It's about testing your most important hypothesis:

"Will someone care enough to take action?"

Not compliment it.

Not nod politely.

Not saying, "That's cool."

But *by doing* something, through action.

Click it. Buy it. Sign up. Share and Engage.

That's the kind of proof you're chasing.

Because once someone takes action, you're no longer guessing. You're learning. And, learning is where the momentum lives.

What MVPs Are Really About: Velocity and Validation?

A good MVP should have these five attributes:

1. **Fast** to build (think hours or days, not months)

2. **Focused** on one problem, one audience, one outcome

3. **Functional** enough to display value even if it's scrappy

4. **Flexible** so you can iterate later based on the feedback

5. **Feedback-driven** because opinions aren't data, but behavior is

You don't just beat perfectionists to the punch when you ship it out early. You get real-world clarity they'll never have. Also, it is because you're in motion, and motion creates traction.

10 Real-World MVP Strategies

Here are ten MVP methods used by smart entrepreneurs to validate their ideas with speed and precision:

1. The Landing Page Test

Build a single page that describes your offer, showcases the benefits, and ends with a clear call-to-action.

Want signups? Add a waitlist form.

Want sales? Add a pre-order button.

Track the clicks. Watch the behavior. Learn from what resonates.

If they won't click a button, they won't pull out a wallet either.

2. The MVP Form

Instead of building a platform, build a custom form.

Do you want to create a personalized fitness app? Generate a form that asks users about their goals, then send them customized plans and offers.

You're testing the outcome, not the automation.

If they love the result, you've proven demand. Now you can scale.

3. The Concierge Model

Act as the product.

You want to build a job-matching app? First, match people manually. Then, you may want to create an AI-based content tool? Write the content yourself using the same logic the tool would.

You learn the pain points. You see the friction. You are feeling what your users feel. Now it's time to get to work. Sweat before scaling.

4. The Clickable Prototype

Create interactive demos without writing a single line of code.

You can simulate a full product experience right from login to checkout and be able to test user reactions.

People are not looking for a novel idea. But they are looking for something that they want, which will help them simplify their lives.

5. The Product Drop

Create a brand. Post mockups on a few field-tested social media platforms. Build a vibe.

See if people are DM-ing you.

See if people are asking, "Where can I buy this?"

You don't need an inventory. You don't need e-commerce.

You need curiosity and a boatload of comments and testimonials.

If it gains attention before it exists, you've got a winner.

6. The Paid Beta Version

Offer early access by charging a reduced price. Make it exclusive, Intimate, and Personal. Gather feedback. Refine fast. Now you're making money *and* building something that people want. If they're willing to pay while it's imperfect, you've struck a nerve.

7. The Walkthrough

Record a demo. Narrate your idea. Walk users through your proposed solution step-by-step. Then post it. Send it to your list.

Show it to all your prospects.

Only then, ask them this question: "Would this save you time or money?" Then wait for their answer. Their eyes, their questions, and their expressions will give you all the answers you need.

8. The Stack

You don't need codes, but you need outcomes.

Stitch together a functioning prototype of different functionality apps. They are not glamorous. They don't scale, but they work.

Real results beat elegant interfaces every time.

9. The Fake Product Drop

Post a mock launch. Collect pre-orders. If enough people buy, then fulfill it. If not, give them a refund. Twist, Tweak, and Repeat, until you get it right. Then start charging premium prices for your product's uniqueness.

Using this method, you've validated your product in the marketplace without spending a single dime on manufacturing.

Create Demand first. Then deliver as promised.

10. The Community Test

Create a space. Invite people. Let them talk. Observe their needs. Ask better questions. When they start venting, listen.

When they start asking, build.

The Community displays the clearest mirror, displaying any signs of pain, where its feelings and wants are untainted. They are authentic in their true self and hold their principles to much higher standards.

MVPs Aren't the End: They're the Entry Point

Don't confuse your MVP with your final product.

Your first version is a flashlight in the dark. It shows you where to go next.

Sometimes it'll help you succeed. Sometimes you will flop. But either way, you'll know more today than you did yesterday.

That's progress.

That's validation.

That's proof that you're in the game.

And that puts you ahead of the 99% of wannabe founders who still have their ideas stuck in their heads and don't know how to get them out to the marketplace.

THE EXCESSES OF
WEALTH

THE PLIGHT OF
POVERTY

CHAPTER 9

Positioning Your Solution

"Don't sell your product. Sell the better version of your customers' present life. Most importantly, sell them the benefits and the results they expect."

The difference between something that sells once and something that sells for years *is not just the solution itself.* It's how the solution is positioned in the customer's mind.

Let's get something clear:

- You're not in the business of features.

- You're in the business of felt outcomes.

If you can package your solution as:

- Easier than how it is currently

- Emotionally relieving

- More valuable to them

Then you won't just win sales. You'll win loyalty.

The Human Test: Would a Stranger Understand This in just 7 Seconds?

Let's say your solution is a tool that automates client emails. You then start marketing it in one of these two ways:

1. You could say that it automates client workflows. Or

2. You could say that it gives you your evenings back by writing and sending emails for you.

Both are the same in their functionality. But the difference lies in their packaging and presentation. How it is presented and portrayed matters a lot.

Guess which one will sell like hotcakes?

The second one. Always.

Because it speaks directly to the customer, the life he or she wants to live, and not the tool he or she will use to get there. Your packaging should scream, and they should say, *"This is the thing I've been looking for,"* even if they didn't know what to name it or what to call it, but they want it.

Pointers to Great Positioning

1. Make It Relatable, Not Technical

No jargon. Just pain-relief language.

People will buy what they truly understand.

2. Connect It to an Outcome They Already Crave

Connect them to the future they envision.

Tap into the desires they already feel.

Show them the outcome: More time. More freedom. Less frustration. More control.

3. Wrap It Up in a Promise That Feels Real

No need for hype. Just clarity.

You may say: "Turn your 3-hour-long ordeal into just 10 minutes of work to get the job done, with just one click."

Who would not want that?

You do not want to sound too technical, such as: "Revolutionize your operations through intelligent synergy."

The "One-Liner" Formula

Here's a simple formula that works across any industry:

"We help [specific person] achieve [specific outcome] without [common frustration]."

For example:

"We help Contractors get high-paying clients without spending hours on writing multiple proposals."

This one sentence becomes your positioning anchor. Market it on your site, in your DMs, in your pitch, and on every article of your marketing materials. It does the heavy lifting for you because it focuses on who, what, and why it matters. It also conveys the message faster, in its crispness and clarity.

Make Your Solution Look Bigger Than It Is

Early on, perception matters more than scale. If your tool is simple but focused- don't hide that. Highlight it. If your system is small but mighty, package it with boldness and specificity.

Simplicity sells when it looks **intentional**.

Never say "I'm just starting out."

Instead, say it differently: "We specialize in solving this one painful problem, fast."

That clarity and precision? That's premium energy.

And people don't pay more for size. They pay more for certainty.

Package It to Be Valuable, Scalable, and Impactful.

Your solution's value shouldn't be just in what it does, but in how it feels. A $1o/lb grapes can feel like a $10,000 experience when it is packaged right with a real story behind it. Such as mentioning on its packaging where it is grown, how it got here from miles away, and showcasing its uniqueness in the marketplace.

This story can help create imagination and can increase its perceptive value. Your MVP needs that same magic. Package it so it screams relief, not features.

A designer built a tool to help small businesses track invoices. Instead of selling a "software program", she sold it using this captivating caption: "Never Lose Sleep Over Unpaid Bills Again." This caught everyone's attention. She added a one-page setup guide and a 30-day money-back promise. Suddenly, her $50 tool felt like a lifeline worth $500. This simple promise may have boosted her sales exponentially in a relatively short time.

Scalability should be your next move. Your solution should grow in tandem with your customers' needs. A tutor helping kids with math didn't stop at one-on-one sessions.

She packaged her approach by taking it into group classes, then an online course, and then a subscription for weekly practice sheets. This takes time and patience to evolve. Each step solved the same pain kids felt when falling behind, but she was able to reach more people without working any harder. That's scalability: one solution, many wallets, and multiple income streams.

Impact comes from outcomes, not outputs. People are not buying your app, your coaching, or your guides, but they are buying what it does for them. Namely, the outputs they desire. Frame your solution around the transformation.

Create with this in mind: How can my product or service help them? Make it clear, make it vivid, make it theirs, and make them come back for more of your products and services. You may try these out and find that you, too, may be on your way to becoming stinking rich in your own way.

CHAPTER 10

Pricing the Problem, Not the Product

Here's where the rubber meets the road. If you want to get stinking rich, stop pricing your solution like it's a yard sale. A $20 app might solve a $20,000 problem. A $1,000 coaching package might save a business $100,000. The secret to big money is pricing based on the pain you erase, not the product you sell. Let's get deeper into this.

Let's get something straight:

People don't pay you for what you build. They pay you for what it solves. For the relief, for the result, for the weight it lifts off their shoulders.

That's why you should never price based on your effort or the product. You price it based on *pain, the pain it helps relieve,* and how deeply your product or service helps remove it.

Don't just say: "It took me 6 months to build this. So, I deserve to charge more."

Say instead: "This solves a $500,000-a-month problem for the business I am selling my solution to. Hence, my charge is based on the impact it is making for the company."

In the end, people don't reward you for your hard work, but they reward you for helping them with their own transformation.

The Psychology of Pricing

Pricing isn't just math, it's human nature. People don't buy features; they buy escape, hope, and results. The family whose house was burnt doesn't care how many gallons of water were used by the firefighters to extinguish the flames; all they care about is that their life was saved. Your solution is that water. The pricing should be based on the life it saves, not on how the firetruck filled with water came into the scenario.

Take the example of a small business owner drowning in customer complaints. Lackluster ROI, lack of visibility and publicity, and lost sales-it's killing her. A consultant offers her a $15,000 system to streamline her customer service that could potentially bring in 3X income for her. It may cut the complaints she receives by half, saving her $65,000 a year in lost revenue. She doesn't and will not blink at the $15,000 investment into her business.

Why? Because the pain she has is much louder than the price. Your job is to make that math clear: show them what they're losing, then show them what you're saving them. This can help put things in perspective.

How Much Pain Are You Solving?

Here's a secret:

If your product solves a *painful, frequent, and urgent* problem, your customer isn't checking for your price tag.

They will be asking: "Where have you been all my life?" "I have been waiting for this solution for a very long time."

People will pay top dollars if:

- You save them time
- You save them energy

- You save them from embarrassment, failure, or fear
- Or you make their life feel much easier instantly

Every possible scenario may play out within these criteria, or in a combination. In some exceptional cases, it may fit outside these boundaries.

Price is not about logic. It's about relief.

If someone has been carrying a heavy burden every day, and you show up with something that takes it off them, they'll pay you what they *feel* it's worth.

Not what you think it's worth.

The Broken Pipe Rule

Picture this:

A pipe bursts.

Water is flooding into the kitchen. You call the plumber. He comes, taps at one spot, tightens one valve, and it stops. 15 minutes top. Then he hands you a $900 bill. You're shocked.

$900 for 15 minutes?!" Now you start questioning his ethics and morality. But an hour ago, you were ready to pay him any amount he asked.

He smiles:

"No. $1 was for my time. $899 was for knowing *where* to tap."

That's pricing the problem, not the product.

How to Set Your Price Like a Problem-Solver?

Here's a quick framework:

1. **Understand the value of the result.**

2. What will this help the user achieve that's meaningful to them?

3. **Think of the cost of the problem staying unresolved.**

4. What's it costing them *not* to have this resolved right now? Will it cost them more as time passes and the damage assessment broadens?

5. **Price based on urgency, frustration, and frequency.**

6. If it's a constant pain, price confidently.

7. **Never discount your power.**

8. Simplicity isn't "cheap." Simplicity is genius. Charge fairly.

Pricing Scenarios showing examples

Problem	Solution	Value	Price You Could Charge
Losing 10 hours per week formatting reports	Simple formatting tool	Saves 40 hrs/month	$5,000 per month
Spending 4 days trying to format manuscripts	Post-ready templates	Reduces mental fatigue and stress	$3,500
HR spending for onboarding staff: 2 Hours per day	Onboarding automation	Saves weeks/year	$10,200

Parents are stressed out and yelling every morning	Morning prep assistant	Restores family peace	$8,700

Don't be afraid to price high.

What feels "small" to you might feel like a total breakthrough to them.

The Final Rule: Price with Courage

If your product solves a painful problem, you deserve to price it boldly.

Not with arrogance but with clarity.

If someone says, "That's expensive,"

You can calmly respond:

"Compared to what this saves you in time, stress, and sanity, it's actually a great deal." That will help put matters to rest.

The truth behind all this is:

The price becomes a mere footnote when you help solve a valuable problem well in all its splendor.

PART 3
MONETIZING LIKE A BILLIONAIRE

CHAPTER 11

Business Models That Print Cash

Big solutions are great. But bigger solutions that pay you repeatedly? That's how you build a business that breathes without you. Ideas don't make money, models do.

If you're going to solve real pain, then it's only fair you get paid well and match the value you help deliver. A powerful business model doesn't just make you rich; it makes your solution sustainable. It funds your growth, fuels your team, and helps buy back your time.

Why Business Models Matter?

A great solution in itself is only half the game. The wrong model can trap you inside the hamster wheel. You will be working harder and harder for every dollar while inflation erodes from the other side. You will not see it or hear it.

But the right model can set you free. Your goal is to solve the same big problems for more people, more often, and without burning out. Let's break this down into the business models that have stood the test of time, not by luck, but by solving pain at scale and capturing value continuously, seamlessly, and effortlessly.

1. SaaS (Software as a Service)

Imagine building a product once and having people pay you monthly to keep using it perpetually. But, for it to be and to stay perpetual, it needs to be an evergreen problem, such as waste management. Humans will always be creating waste. Wastegeneration is here to stay. That will be an ideal and perfect business when taken into context.

Now, back to a virtual software product, SaaS. You take a problem people face every day-something repeatable, trackable, and painful—and you build a digital tool to help solve it. The cost to deliver to each new user is low. The value you provide is ongoing. This may work well in a subscription model with predictable monthly cash flow.

You don't just sell software. You sell *relief on autopilot.*

Think: A dashboard that helps households track invoices, or a platform that schedules meetings across time zones. These are not flashy businesses—they're friction killers. And people will pay to get rid of that friction from their lives.

2. Consulting

Sometimes, people don't want a tool to work with. They want it completely hands-off. They want to use your brain power. This is power on steroids, filled with wisdom, experience, and expertise all in one package.

If you've cracked a system that works—marketing, hiring, scaling, or negotiation- you can start monetizing your thinking. Consulting lets you step in, analyze someone's mess, and help them fix it.

But here's the key: people don't pay for advice. They pay for clarity and a solution.

They pay to skip mistakes, fast-track results, and feel safe in uncertain terrain. If you become the person who "makes sense of things to them," consulting then becomes your golden ladder.

3. Licensing

Let's say you build a solution, probably an invention, a course, a framework, a tech, or a product. What if others could use your IP under their brand, in their company, to help propel their company to the next level or beat out competitors in a competitive marketplace?

That's done by licensing your product.

You don't have to be everywhere. You just need to *build once*, and let others pay to use it repeatedly. Licensing turns your system into an asset that works while you sleep.

Think of it as renting your brilliance. This is your virtual asset.

4. Subscription Services

Subscriptions are the most reliable business models for one reason: *predictable monthly revenue.*

You don't have to start from scratch every month. Whether it's curated info, products, communities, or ongoing support—subscriptions create habit loops around your offer.

You become part of their life rhythm. And once you're in that rhythm, you stay funded, focused, and free.

5. Agencies

If people want results without the headache, they'll hire you to "do it for them." Agencies are built on operations, delivery, and client retention. They take expertise and turn it into service, often by managing the full sequence of processes for the client.

This model tends to grow fast, but it needs systems, teams, and standards.

You're not selling time here, you're selling outcomes. When done well, agencies can dominate entire industries by being the go-to execution arm for busy clients.

6. Partnerships

Sometimes, instead of doing everything yourself, you can link up with someone with what you don't: a big audience, a deep network, or complementary services.

You bring the solution. They bring in the crowd. It can be a win-win for both parties involved.

Partnerships are the smart person's shortcut to scale. You don't have to own every piece-just enough of the right-sized pie.

So, which one or more should you choose?

Ask yourself:

- Do I want high margins or high speed?
- Do I want recurring revenue or one-off deals?
- Do I want to be product-based, service-based, or hybrid?

Each model ties to the pain you help solve. SaaS and subscription services may work for ongoing problems (e.g., time management, education). Consulting and agencies may fit professional pain (e.g., business growth). Licensing suits solutions you can package and hand off. There's no perfect model. There is nothing right or wrong. You will need to customize it based on your needs. But the wrong model can drain your energy even with the right product. You must be wary of where you are stepping before venturing into unknown territory.

You may choose the one that matches your strengths, serves your customer's needs, and can scale without burning you out.

OPPOSITE SIDES OF WEALTH

CHAPTER 12

From $100K to $1 Million a Month

Everyone wants to scale, but few build to scale. Most people build for the "now." The instant hit. The viral spike. But real scaling isn't a lucky streak, it's a structured phase of evolution. A staircase, not an elevator.

You're making money. Maybe $100K a year. Nice work. But to get stinking rich, you need to think bigger, upscale to $1 million a *month*. That's not a pipe dream; it's a plan. Scaling from six figures to seven isn't about working harder; it's about working smarter. Think of your business like a campfire. You've got a spark. Now you need to add logs, fan the flames, nurture that flame, and turn it into a bonfire.

Let's talk about how to scale your revenue intelligently.

Phase 1: Survival (0 – $100K/year)
Now, you're proving the problem is real and your solution works.

You're testing everything:

- Who exactly needs this?
- Will they pay?
- How painful is the pain?

You're likely doing the selling yourself. You're talking to customers. You're refining, reshaping, and repackaging the offers.

This is the messy phase. But this is where the gold is. Every conversation is a data point. Every buyer is a case study.

Phase 2: Stability ($100K – $500K/year)

Now, you've found traction. The pain is clear. The market exists.

Here, you systematize. You build delivery processes. You document what works. You start outsourcing low-value tasks. Your job shifts from *doer* to *builder*.

You must resist the urge to chase ten new ideas. You double down. Refine. Clean up the mess behind your momentum and move forward. You keep track of your mistakes and correct them, not by sweeping them under the rug, but to learn from those past mistakes.

Phase 3: Scale ($500K – $1M Plus/year)

This is where structure matters.

You install dashboards.

You implement automation.

You define acquisition channels (ads, referrals, content, etc.).

You focus on customer success because recurring revenue depends on retention. You focus on existing clients and cater to all their needs. On the side and in parallel, you work on bringing on new ones.

You stop asking, "How do I sell more?" and start asking, "How do I make this run without me?" For this to happen, you must have systems, processes, and manpower.

And this is where *Recurring Revenue Engines* come in.

What's a Recurring Revenue Engine?

It's a setup where income keeps flowing automatically *without starting from zero at the start of each month.* The real money is seen in recurring revenue, cash that flows in monthly without begging for it. Subscriptions, memberships, and retainers are your driver of these massive and foolproof engines.

Here are a few examples:

- A software tool set on a monthly plan.

- A paid membership community with freshly input monthly content.

- A service with a retainer structure.

- A product subscription box that surprises and delights.

These engines turn today's work into tomorrow's income.

You want your life to feel like compound interest, which compounds and scales as years and decades pass. Every action builds momentum.

When you build engines that are scalable and sustainable, you buy freedom. You can also buy back time through the power of delegation. And how do you do that? When you buy freedom, you buy back your time.

CHAPTER 13

Marketing That Converts Pain into Profit

Marketing isn't about flashy ads or viral stunts; it's about finding people drowning in pain and showing them your life raft. Your marketing must stop sounding like an elevator pitch and start sounding like a rescue. They are not looking for your marketing, but are looking for a solution to their problems.

Now, let's build the kind of marketing that converts pain into profit.

Start With Problem-Aware Buyers

You don't need to educate everyone. Start with those who *already feel the pain.*

They're the ones typing into search bars.

They're complaining in the comment sections.

They're asking friends for help.

Your job? It is to show where they are with one simple message: "This doesn't have to hurt anymore. I have the solution to your problem."

When you speak the customer's frustration fluently, they lean in. When you describe their struggle better than they can, they trust you have the cure. You will need to find a mutual way to connect with them through their pain and your experience with your product (in the middle), which is the tool you are offering them as the solution to their problem.

The Art of Converting Pain

Converting isn't about pushing, it's about pulling. People act when they feel understood. That professional who is suffering from intense pain does not want to buy a course; all she wants is her life back. Show your customers that you see their struggles and you understand them. You may use illustrations as examples: "One parent went from frazzled to focused with our planning tool." Use guarantees: "Get organized in a week or get your money back. No questions asked." Use clarity: "This helps solve your sleepless nights, not just your schedule."

A tutor helping kids with math doesn't sell "lessons." She sells "confidence in class." Her funnel, a free study guide, a $10 workshop, and a $200 course, speaks directly to the parents of kids who fear their kids falling behind. By the time she pitched the course, they were begging to sign up. That's conversion: meeting pain with hope, step by step.

Build a Simple, High-Trust Funnel

Here's what it works:

1. **A Hook That Hits a Nerve**
2. "Sick of wasting time doing XYZ the hard way?"
3. **A Promise That Calms the Pain**
4. "Here's how to fix it in 10 minutes or less."
5. **Proof That It Works**
6. Screenshots. Testimonials. And most importantly, Results.

7. **A Path to Say Yes**

8. Easy checkout. No guesswork.

Marketing isn't about pressure. It's about clarity. When the offer is obvious, people stop scrolling and pay attention.

ROI Math: Make the Numbers Work

If your product is $100 and your customer stays for 6 months, your LTV (lifetime value) is $600.

Now, imagine you spend $200 to acquire that customer.

You just earned $600 with an investment of $200.

This is not advertising. This is math. When the numbers work, scaling becomes science—not luck.

RICHES FROM THE FIRST DRIP

Chapter 14

Big Problems →
Big Solutions → Big Profits

In college, I used to chase small wins $100 for a quick gig, $200 a day for an odd job, thinking that quantity could lead me to wealth. I was wrong. It didn't. I was busy, stressed, and still broke. Then I discovered a truth that flipped my world: When you solve big problems, you can unlock much bigger profits. The bigger the pain you relieve, the bigger the solution you have to offer, and the bigger the paycheck will be waiting for you on the other side.

Millionaires and billionaires don't dabble in trivial fixes. They target problems that cripple businesses or lives, deliver game-changing solutions, and charge what the impact demands. This isn't about grinding harder—it's about choosing problems that matter most and turning them into wealth. Here's how to identify massive problems, craft transformative solutions, and cash in on the value you create.

The Profit Potential of Big Problems

Small problems pay small. If you're fixing typos on a website, you might earn a quick $50, but it's not life-changing for anyone. Big problems, when faced by a large company that is losing millions to supply chain delays or a small business hemorrhaging money each month, they are willing to pay top dollars to find a quick fix. At this point, they are not shopping for price, but finding immediate solutions. These scenarios are urgent and costly. People will pay a fortune to help solve them.

I saw this transformation happen in one company, which made the shift from generic IT support to preventing, handling, and fixing cybersecurity breaches for mid-sized firms. A website tweak might earn them $200; preventing a $1,000,000 data breach earned them $50,000 per contract. Big problems command big fees because they deliver big relief. The formula is clear: find high-stakes problems, find a fix, and the profits will follow.

Hunting for High-Impact Problems

Big problems aren't always obvious; you have to hunt for them. I used to think any client need was worth solving, but I was wrong. A content manager spent weeks helping a startup with their social media captions, only to realize they'd pay more to fix their chaotic customer onboarding process. Big problems hurt deeply and demand immediate and urgent action.

Here's how to find them:

Eavesdrop on Pain: Dive into industry chats, media threads, and coffee shop conversations. To illustrate with an example: A consultant noticed many logistics companies venting about delivery delays costing them clients, which was my signal to learn more about it.

Measure the Stakes: Ask, "What's this problem costing money, time, and reputation?" Delivery delays were costing firms $10,000 a week in lost contracts.

Spot the Urgency: Big problems are urgent; people can't wait to fix them. Logistics managers were desperate for solutions because delays were killing their credibility.

Validate with a Probe: The consultant offers a low-cost pilot program to test interest. He proposed a $200 delivery tracking plan to one company, and when it saved them $8,000 in a month, he knew that he had hit a nerve.

Look for specific problems that affect many—like "streamlining logistics for e-commerce" versus "helping businesses grow." The right problem is your ticket to wealth.

Crafting Solutions That Transform

A big problem needs a big solution, one that delivers measurable impact and feels like a lifeline. When he tackled logistics delays, he didn't just suggest better software. He built a custom dashboard that helps track shipments in real-time, flags delays, and automates client updates. The result? His client cut delays by 60% and held onto their biggest accounts.

How to create solutions that sell?

Here's how to create solutions that sell:

Target the Core Issue: Don't slap on a temporary solution and walk off thinking it will fix the problem. The consultant found delays stemmed from poor communication between drivers and warehouses, so his solution fixed that missing link.

Keep It Accessible: Big solutions don't need to be complex. In this case, his dashboard was simple enough for any manager to use, which made it a must-have.

Show Immediate Value: Deliver a quick win to prove your worth. His client saw a 20% drop in delays within two weeks, which sealed their trust.

Build for Scale: Ensure your solution grows with the problem. His dashboard worked for one warehouse but could handle 50, making it more valuable as the company expanded.

A transformative solution turns you from a vendor into a partner. Clients won't just pay you—they'll rely on you.

How to turn solutions into profit?

Here's how to turn solutions into profits:

Price the Impact: Charge based on the value you deliver, not your work hours. If you save a client $100,000, a $20,000 fee is a bargain and no-brainer. He tied his pricing structure to the revenue he generated for his clients.

Create Recurring Revenue: Offer ongoing support and possibly subscriptions. His maintenance plan kept clients hooked and his income steady.

Leverage Success Stories: Share your results to attract bigger fish. After one client saved $30,000, he posted a case study, landing two new contracts worth $25,000 each.

Negotiate Confidently: Don't undervalue yourself. When a client pushed back on his $25,000 fee, he showed them the cost of their delays, which amounted to over $900,000 annually. Once they had the proof in black and white, they signed on the spot without any hesitation.

Big profits come from imparting massive impact. Make sure to show your clients the cost of not hiring you, and only then will your price become a no-brainer.

The Momentum of Big Wins

Solving big problems doesn't just bring cash; it builds a flywheel. After streamlining logistics for one company, he became "the go-to guy." Referrals poured in, and he landed contracts with much bigger firms at $100,000 a pop.

His reputation grew, his confidence soared, and new opportunities opened, such as speaking at industry events.

Big solutions also create trust. Clients who saw his results recommended him to others; one even partnered with him on a logistics tech startup. Solving a big problem doesn't just fill your wallet; it builds a new platform ripe for exponential growth and scale.

PART 4

BRANDING YOURSELF AS A PROBLEM SOLVER: Becoming the Go-To Expert by Focusing on One Specialty

CHAPTER 15

Own One Problem, Master One Niche

I used to think getting rich meant chasing every opportunity, offering every service, and jumping on every trend. In my younger days, I was hopeful, doing everything from being an assistant to copywriting, hoping to catch a big break. But I was barely scraping by, overworked and unnoticed. Clients didn't see me as special; I was just another hustler in a crowded market. Then I realized the secret to wealth: solve one specific, high-value problem better than anyone else, and become the go-to person for it. That's how you get rich owning one problem and mastering one niche.

Millionaires don't try to fix everything for everybody. They zero in on a single pain point that people pay for to help solve, and they build their fortune around it. Focusing on one problem creates clarity, builds trust, and attracts clients ready to pay premium prices. Here's how to get rich by solving one high-value problem and dominating your niche.

Why One Focused Problem Leads to Wealth?

When I struggled, I thought offering more services would bring more money. I was wrong. People don't pay for "everything"; they pay for solutions to their specific headaches. The sharper your focus, the more valuable you become. Think about it: if your business is bleeding cash, you don't want a generic consultant; you want the expert who lives and breathes cash flow fixes daily.

Let's now evaluate the journey of a restaurant consultant who went from being a general "business coach" to specializing in helping restaurants boost profit margins. He became the guy owners call first by focusing on one problem: low margins in a tough industry. Within a year, he was charging $50,000 per client and had a waiting list. Why? Because he owned their problem, that kept restaurant owners up at night. Solving one high-value problem makes you indispensable, and that's where the money flows.

Finding the Right Problem to Solve

Not every problem is a goldmine. To get rich, you need a pain point that's urgent, expensive, and widespread. Early on, a freelancer wasted ample time offering low-value services like social media posts for startups with no budget. The real money came when he focused on helping small businesses stabilize their cash flow, a problem they'd pay thousands to fix.

How to find a high-value problem?

Listen to the Market: Dive into forums, posts, threads, and conversations in forums where your target audience vents their concerns and complaints. He found small business owners ranting about unpredictable revenue and late payments. That was his cue.

Quantify the Pain: Ask, "How much is this problem costing them?" If it's draining their time, profits, or sanity, it's likely worth solving. Cash flow issues were costing his clients thousands of dollars monthly.

Test the Demand: Offer a small solution, a consultation, a guide, or a quick fix and see who bites. He created a $99 cash flow checklist and sold 115 in a week, proving the problem was real.

The best problems are specific but common. "Helping Nurses manage taxes" beats "helping people with money." Find a pain point that's both a niche and in demand, and you're halfway to wealth.

Master the Solution

Owning a problem means being the best at solving it. When he zeroed in on cash flow, he didn't just offer generic advice. He studied accounting basics, mastered forecasting tools, and created templates that saved his clients hours. They didn't just hire him; they trusted him because he delivered results no one else could.

To master your niche and get rich:

Go Deep: Learn everything about your problem. He took a $200 accounting course and read three books on cash flow management. That knowledge let him charge 5x more than the general consultants. Invest in yourself first.

Deliver Results: Start with small wins to build trust. He offered free cash flow audits to five businesses, fixed their issues, and turned four into paying clients at $2,000 each.

Build Authority: Share your expertise through content—blogs, videos, and posts. He posted weekly cash flow tips on his blogs, which led to a client who paid $7,000 for a single project.

Stay Focused: Say no to projects outside your niche. Turning down a $500 logo job may feel scary, but it freed him up to land a $5,000 cash flow contract. Set your priorities.

Mastery isn't about being perfect; it's about being the most reliable solution. The better you help solve the problem, the more people will be ready to pay you.

Be Known as the Problem-Solver

You can't get rich if no one knows you're the expert. Early on, he was terrified of self-promotion, worried he'd seem pushy. But staying invisible kept him broke. Millionaires don't wait for clients to find them; they make sure their name is synonymous with the solution. That's where the tie-up happens.

Here's how to be known for:

Share Your Why: Tell a story about why you are helping solve this problem. In this example, he shared his struggles with cash flow as a freelancer, which helped him connect with business owners and build trust.

Showcase Wins: Highlight results with case studies and testimonials. After helping a client save $15,000, he shared their story (with permission), bringing in three new clients.

Target Your Audience: Focus on where your clients are. He joined various online and offline communities for entrepreneurs and local business groups. This helped him land speaking opportunities in speaker circuits, which led to $70,000 in revenue.

Stay Consistent: Show up regularly with value. One post a week about cash flow on his blog helped him grow his following and brought in new clients.

Being known isn't about being loud; it's about being the name people think of when they face that particular problem for which you are specialized. That's when the money starts rolling in.

The Wealth of Owning One Problem

When you own one problem and master one niche, the game changes. Clients seek you out. You get to charge premium rates. You work less to create more impact. After focusing on cash flow solutions, he went from earning $20,000 a month to $100K a month, all because he came to be known as the person who can fix that problem. His reputation grew, referrals poured in, and he could finally breathe.

Owning a problem doesn't lock you in; it's your launchpad. Once you dominate one niche, you can expand or pivot with credibility. But you must start here: pick one high-value pain point, master the solution, and ensure the world knows you're the expert. Solve that problem better than anyone else, and the wealth will follow today and for years to come.

DESIGN THE LANDCRAFT THAT SCAPES

CHAPTER 16

Build a Magnetic Personal Brand

Your brand is your story, lived out loud. It's how you show up, the problems you solve, and the people you touch. It also encompasses every honest moment you share, every connection you nurture, and every promise you keep. Building a brand that's not just seen but felt. You're not just building a business, you're building a presence that pulls people in, lifts them, and pays you back in wealth, trust, and freedom.

To Get Stinking Rich Solving Others' Problems, you need to do that with your voice, which is your brand. Not by blasting polished taglines or flexing a curated life. A magnetic personal brand doesn't shout; it hums. It pulls people in with your raw, authentic, real story, wins, stumbles, and inner fire.

Why Your Brand Is Your Superpower?

Your brand isn't a logo or a slick bio, it's the vibe people catch when your name comes up. It's the trust you spark, the story you live, and the value you deliver, all wrapped in a presence unmistakably *you*. In this journey of building riches through solving problems, your brand is the bridge that connects your solutions to the folks who need them. Clients pick you over the next guy, partners knock on your door, and people rally behind your mission.

A magnetic brand doesn't just grab attention, it holds it. It turns strangers into die-hard supporters, doubters into believers, and one-off gigs into lifelong relationships. It's not about looking flawless or chasing clout; it's about showing up as the real you, flaws, fire, and all together. This makes you authentically genuine. When you build a brand that resonates, you're not just selling a service—you're sharing a promise, backed by your truth.

Why be authentic and own your identity?

Never be an imposter. Create your identity, which will help you stand out from the crowd. There is only one of you on this planet. Make it count. It's easy to fall into the trap of mimicking those picture-perfect influencers with glossy shots and rehearsed one-liners. But a brand built on a fake front is like a shiny balloon. One wrong prick, and it pops. People can sniff out a poser from miles away. They don't vibe with airbrushed highlight reels; they connect with real, messy, and real human moments.

You're just adding to the noise if you're chasing likes or trying to be someone you're not. A magnetic brand whispers your truth and makes people lean in. It draws them in.

How to Build a Brand That Sticks?

Crafting a magnetic personal brand is like telling a story people can't stop listening to. It's about rooting it in real life, experiences, hardships, sharing your battle scars, and showing where it counts. Here's how to make it happen:

1. Root Your Brand in Your Real Story

Your brand starts with your truth, the raw, unfiltered moments that have shaped you. People don't fall for products; they fall for the dreams, struggles, and victories behind them.

- **Dig Up Your Spark**: Think back to the moment that lit your fire. Was it the night you sat at your kitchen table, heart racing, realizing your side hustle was your shot at breaking free? Or the gut-punch of being told to "stick to the safe path" when you knew you were built for more? It was the moment I saw my first job wasn't satisfying and found myself clawing my way out of it to seek freedom. That story is my brand's pulse. That fire in the belly has given me the courage to listen to my instincts and follow my dreams.

- **Share the Bites and Sharpness**: Don't smooth out the rough edges. Talk about the sleepless nights, the doubts that kept you up, the defiance that pushed you forward despite the cold nights when you went hungry. A baker might share how their first failed cake led to a recipe that won competitions and delighted the taste buds. A coach might talk about hitting rock bottom before helping others rise. That's what makes your brand stick like glue. There is a sense of connectedness that pulls people in.

- **Weave It Everywhere**: Let your story seep into every interaction: your pitch, posts, and client chats. Make it the thread that ties your brand together.

2. Show Your Scars, Not Just Your Shine

Nobody trusts a know-it-all with a perfect track record. Flaws give out authenticity and genuineness. But when you open up about your stumbles and your fears, people let their guard down and tend to accept you the way you are. But when you portray yourself as someone you are not, all the red flags go up in their minds. You become someone they can relate to when you show your true colors in full splendor, and now you become someone they can trust.

- **Own Your Mess-Ups**: Talk about when you lost a big client, botched a project, or almost threw in the towel or closed shop. Everyone falls, and we learn with each misstep. We learn from each other's triumphs and tribulations when we open up to sharing our positive and negative experiences. It opened doors to real talks and new opportunities.

- **Highlight the Comeback**: Don't just stop at when you fell and got back up. What did you learn? How did it contribute to who you are today? How did it mold you? Has it made you much stronger both mentally and physically? What did you learn from your battle wounds and defeats? What about setbacks and missteps? I have learned a lot from all of them. What to do and what not to do? Whom to trust and whom not to? Humans will learn at each turn during our journey through life. We will need to imbibe everything and then take the best of what everything has to offer. As with the other side, take it with a grain of salt and learn from what it teaches you.

- **Keep It Real, Not Overdone**: Honesty isn't about airing all your dirty laundry. It's about sharing truths that matter. Be open, but keep it purposeful and simple. Share to lift others, not to dwell on your troubles and victories won.

3. Show Up in the Trenches, Not on a Stage

A brand isn't built by preaching to a faceless crowd; it's forged in real, human connections. Stop treating people like an audience and start meeting them where they are, at ground level and at the level their eyes meet. In reality, no one is superior or inferior to anyone. We will all eventually end up in the same place. Cut out the excess baggage and all the external noise in your life to have a peaceful existence on this planet, which we rent for a short while. Soon our time will come to vacate.

176

- **Be a Real Person**: Reply to comments, answer questions, jump into chats in your niche. If someone shares a struggle online, offer a quick tip, not a sales pitch. Your warmth helps build trust.

- **Hang Out Beyond Your Bubble**: Drop into other people's spaces, comment on posts, join discussions, and show up at virtual meetups if you like to. A consultant might add value to a thread about industry headaches, sparking a conversation that can lead you to getting a new client. Anything is possible. Hey, you never know.

- **Focus on Relationships, Not Numbers**: Aim for one meaningful connection a day, a message to a potential business partner, a thank-you to a client, a nod to a colleague. These moments stack up and turn into genuine influence, meaningful relationships, and networking connections. This takes time to grow and some nurturing to build trust.

4. Send Signals, Not Static

Your brand doesn't need to be loud; it needs to be steady and true.

Think of it like a heartbeat, that is both silent and vital. You do not have to use a megaphone.

- **Pick One Way to Shine**: You don't need to be everywhere. Choose one way to show up by writing a weekly post, recording a short audio clip, or sharing a quick video. A story about a lesson you learned or a client win can pull people in. These can help people connect with you.

- **Share What Hits Home**: Skip the generic stuff. Talk about what stirs you, a customer's breakthrough, a mistake that humbled you, a moment that flipped your perspective. That's what cuts through the clutter and helps you stand out from the crowd.

- **Stay Quietly Bold**: You don't need to yell to lead. A simple story that tells your tale about solving a problem or a candid take on your journey speaks louder than many flashy quotes on media platforms. They help attest to you in silence.

5. Let Your Actions Speak the Loudest

Your brand isn't what you promise, it's what you deliver. Every deadline you nail, every client you wow, and every promise you keep helps you build a reputation that can open doors. Underpromise and overdeliver. This makes them think they have received more than they had asked for. This helps raise your brand image and perception in the marketplace. This can help your brand stand for who you are and help channel you towards the vision you have for your brand.

- **Show Up Every Time**: If you say you'll follow up, make sure you do. If you commit to a result, deliver it. A caterer who always delivers hot meals as promised and on time will create a much stronger brand than any advertisement can brag about.

- **Overdeliver Quietly**: Surprise clients with extra value—a quick tip, a bonus resource, a personal touch. A coach might send a follow-up note with a tailored resource, turning a client into a raving fan.

- **Be Your Proof**: Your work is your calling card. Let your results, happy clients, solved problems, and transformed lives do the talking on your behalf, without uttering a single word or posting an advertisement showcasing your accomplishments.

What does building a Magnetic Brand do?

A magnetic brand doesn't just draw people in; it changes them. One honest story can inspire a client to leap. One genuine conversation can spark a partnership. One kept promise can turn a skeptic into a supporter. Your brand is the spark that lights up your wealth, your impact, and your freedom. Everything rests on your shoulders and your brand. Focus on your branding, and the rest will follow.

Consider a small business coach who started by sharing her story of quitting a soul-sucking job to build her path. She posted about her late-night doubts and small wins, replied to every comment warmly, and delivered results that left clients raving. Her brand grew not from flashy ads but from authentic connections. The landscape she created has shaped her in many ways. Clients referred friends, partners sought her out, and her community became her cheerleaders and ambassadors. Today, she's rich in income and life, and has a purpose. To help people transform their lives for the better.

Things to avoid when building your brand

Building a magnetic brand is powerful but tricky. Steer clear of these traps:

1. **Faking the Vibe**: Don't mimic someone else's style or story. Your truth is your edge, own it. Stand by your ideology and beliefs, and be who you are, not who you are not.

2. **Chasing the crowd**: Likes and followers fade, but real connections will last. Focus on impact, and not numbers.

3. **Hiding Your Humanity**: If you only share your wins, you'll seem untouchable at the surface and bogus.

Failures are part of life. Showcase them too and be genuine about it. People will support your honesty and appreciate your genuineness.

4. **Inconsistency**: A brand that shows up sporadically will lose trust. Be steady, even if it's simple. Being consistent in messaging, delivering, and staying your course no matter what builds trust in the long term. You do not have to fake anything. Be consistent and disciplined to deliver what you have promised.

Your First Step to a Magnetic Brand

You don't need a big platform or stardom to start. Start with where you are, your truth, and the willingness to show up.

- **Reflect**: Write down one moment that has helped shape your journey, a struggle, a win, a pivot, etc.

- **Share**: Tell your story in a short post. Keep it raw, simple, and real.

- **Connect**: Reach out to one person in your circle in your niche. Offer a kind word or a small insight. This helps build mutual relationships.

Your brand defines you, what you stand for, and what you can deliver. It speaks of you and about you. It represents you. Nurture, cherish, safeguard it, and grow it.

CHAPTER 17

Reputation Is Your Currency

Your reputation is your currency to *Get Stinking Rich By Solving Others' Problems*. It's the trust you earn, the stories others tell, the doors that open because of who you are. Every promise you keep, every client you delight, every moment you show up, all of these help build a reputation that's not just seen but felt. You're not just solving problems, you're building a legacy of trust that helps fuel your wealth, impact, and ultimately your freedom.

You've built a magnetic personal brand that hums with authenticity and pulls people in with your story and the genuine truth. But your brand is just the initial spark; your reputation is the fire that keeps burning and is sustainable, long after that first impression fades.

Why Your Reputation Is Your Richest Asset?

Your reputation isn't about what you say about yourself, but it's what others say when you're not in the room. It's the trust you've earned, the stories they tell about you, and the confidence they feel when choosing you. In a world where attention is cheap and skepticism is high, reputation is the currency that buys loyalty, referrals, and opportunities. It's the reason a client may pick you over a cheaper competitor. It's also why a partner bets on your vision. That's also why a community rallies behind you. Trust is the invisible bond that binds all of these. When trust is lost, everything is lost. In essence, your reputation depends on trust to be upheld in the marketplace.

A strong reputation doesn't just fuel your business, it protects it. When markets dip, trends shift, or mistakes become inevitable, your reputation is the anchor that can keep you steady and afloat. It's the trust you've banked through every kept promise, every solved problem, and every human connection. And in the journey to getting stinking rich, the asset pays dividends for life.

The Trap of Chasing Shiny Objects Over Substance

It's tempting to chase quick wins with a viral post, a flashy campaign, and a big announcement. But a reputation built on hype is like a sugar rush: it spikes fast and crashes hard. It is also temporary. People don't trust noise, but they will trust consistency. If you're all sizzle and no steak, you'll burn through goodwill faster than you can rebuild it. A reputation that lasts isn't loud; it will be steady, real, and rooted in delivering value and bringing in the expected results every single time.

How to Build a Reputation That Pays?

Your reputation is grown in the small, intentional moments where you show who you are and what you stand for. It's not about grand gestures but consistent, quiet acts of trust that stack up over time. This may take decades to build, and a fraction of a second to lose. Build a solid reputation that is sustainable by nurturing and fueling it every day. Meet with it and have that inner conversation with yourself.

Here's how you may make it happen:

1. Over-deliver Without a Megaphone

The fastest way to build a reputation is to give more than expected and what was asked for, and let your actions do the talking.

- **Go Beyond the Ask**: When a client asks for an earlier and quicker completion date for the project, make sure to accommodate their request and deliver it. Surprise them. They will be thankful and may pass the word along. This may help you procure new clients.

- **Celebrate Others' Wins**: When a team member steps up and gets the job done, don't just nod, but give them public credit in front of the team. Thus, they may feel respected and valued as a productive member of the team. A quick shoutout in a meeting or a thank-you note can turn a worker into a loyal advocate.

- **Keep It Quiet**: Work in silence and don't broadcast. Let your clients tell your story. Stick to your lane, do your thing, and deliver results as promised, and your client's rave review will do wonders for you.

2. Design Moments That Stick

People don't remember contracts; they remember feelings. Craft experiences that leave them floored, not because they're flashy, but because they're heartfelt and Human.

- **Personalize the Start**: kick off a client relationship with a handwritten note or a short video call, "I'm here for you, and how can I help you accomplish your vision for your project?" This sets an early tone of care and compassion. This is also relationship building.

- **Drop Unexpected Value In the Pit**: Halfway through a project, send a bonus resource, a checklist, a quick tip, or a personal encouragement. That can help boost morale, build trust, and help remove barriers.

- **Make It Memorable**: Small touches can be your storytellers and can help market your brand and your reputation. A photographer might include a candid shot with a note saying: "This moment was magic." This may cost the photographer nothing, but it helps build his image and professionalism with a Human element attached, and it becomes the propellant for his reputation.

3. Turn Clients into a Tribe

Your reputation isn't just yours; it's carried by the people you serve. When your clients become your champions, they spread your name farther than any advertisement could. They become your loyal ambassadors.

- **Create Spaces for Connection**: Bring your clients together. Host a virtual coffee chat, a group call, or a casual meetup where they can share their wins and struggles. A consultant might start a monthly "Growth Huddle" for clients to swap ideas and initiate a brainstorming session.

- **Amplify Their Voices**: Let your clients tell their stories. Ask for testimonials and don't be shy about it. Make it easier by sending a one-question prompt such as, "What method that we discussed, did you focus on in your business that has produced results for you?" Share their words (with permission) to show real impact.

- **Build Trust, Not Transactions**: Treat clients like partners. Check in after a project ends, not to sell, but to care and see what was lacking, and then to improve on it.. A quick message like, "How's it going since we wrapped up our last project?" can turn a one-time client into a lifelong advocate. She may voice her opinions and complaints, and suggest possible improvements or tweaks to the current process.

4. Be a Rock in Rough Waters

Reputations shine brightest when times get tough. How you show up in a recession, a crisis, and during a client's troughs will define you. Give a helping hand to uplift and support them, and help them navigate the obstacles.

- **Stand By Your People**: When a client's struggling, offer a little flexibility, a payment plan, make an extra call, or listen to them. A retailer may discount an existing client, who may be hit by hard times.

- **Stay Steady**: Keep delivering, even when the world feels shaky. Consistency during tough moments helps build trust that lasts. A coach who keeps showing up for clients suffering during a downturn will become unforgettable. They will show him their loyalty by being his lifelong customer.

- **Be Human**: Share your challenges, without oversharing. You may write a post about "How navigating a tough month can help you stay afloat until you get back on your feet". This will show your clients that you're in it with them and will help them overcome the crisis they are currently facing.

5. Let Your Word Be Your Bond That Binds

Your reputation hinges on doing what you say you'll do. Every kept promise, every met deadline, and every delivered result is a deposit in your trust bank.

- **Follow Through, Always**: If you commit to a call, a deliverable, or a follow-up, make it happen. An engineer who delivers a project earlier than the set deadline will build a reputation much stronger than any pitch can.

- **Be Clear and Honest**: Don't overpromise to impress. If a project will take two weeks, say so. Underpromise and overdeliver instead. This may help the outcome by sweetening relationships and taking them to the next level.

- **Own Mistakes Fast**: If you mess up, admit it, fix it, and make it right. A designer who sends a wrong file and corrects it with a bonus touch earns more trust than one who dodges blame. Be upfront and straightforward.

What does building a Rock-Solid Reputation do?

Your reputation isn't just yours. It's a living story told by everyone you touch. One client's word-of-mouth referral can spark ten more referrals. One heartfelt gesture can turn a skeptic into a fan. One moment of standing tall in a crisis can make you a legend. Your reputation doesn't just build your business; it helps build your legacy, your wealth, and your freedom.

What to Avoid when building your reputation?

Building a reputation that pays is powerful but not foolproof. Watch out for these traps:

1. **Chasing Quick Wins**: A viral moment might feel good temporarily, but it soon fades. Focus on providing steady, real value over flash results.

2. **Neglecting the Small Stuff**: Missing a deadline or ignoring a client's concern can dent your reputation. Every moment and its corresponding action counts.

3. **Being All Things to All People**: You can't please everyone. Focus on serving your core clients well. Do not chase every opportunity that comes your way. Streamline your business and focus on what matters..

4. **Forgetting to Listen**: Your reputation grows when you listen to your clients' needs. Don't assume. Always ask and act based on what is said.

Your First Step to a Reputation That Pays

You don't need a big fanfare; you just need a commitment to show up and deliver.

- **Reflect**: Focus on one client to interact with this week. Make their experience exceptional. Ask yourself: How can I make this meeting unforgettable by giving value to my client?

- **Act**: Surprise one person with a small, thoughtful gesture. It may be a thank-you note or something kind.

- **Connect**: Reach out to a past client or colleague. Ask how they're doing and catch up, or share a quick insight with your vendor.

A small act of kindness will be remembered much more than an expensive gift of chocolates or a fruit basket. This may help sow the seed of a reputation that may pave the path for new opportunities and other business relationships.

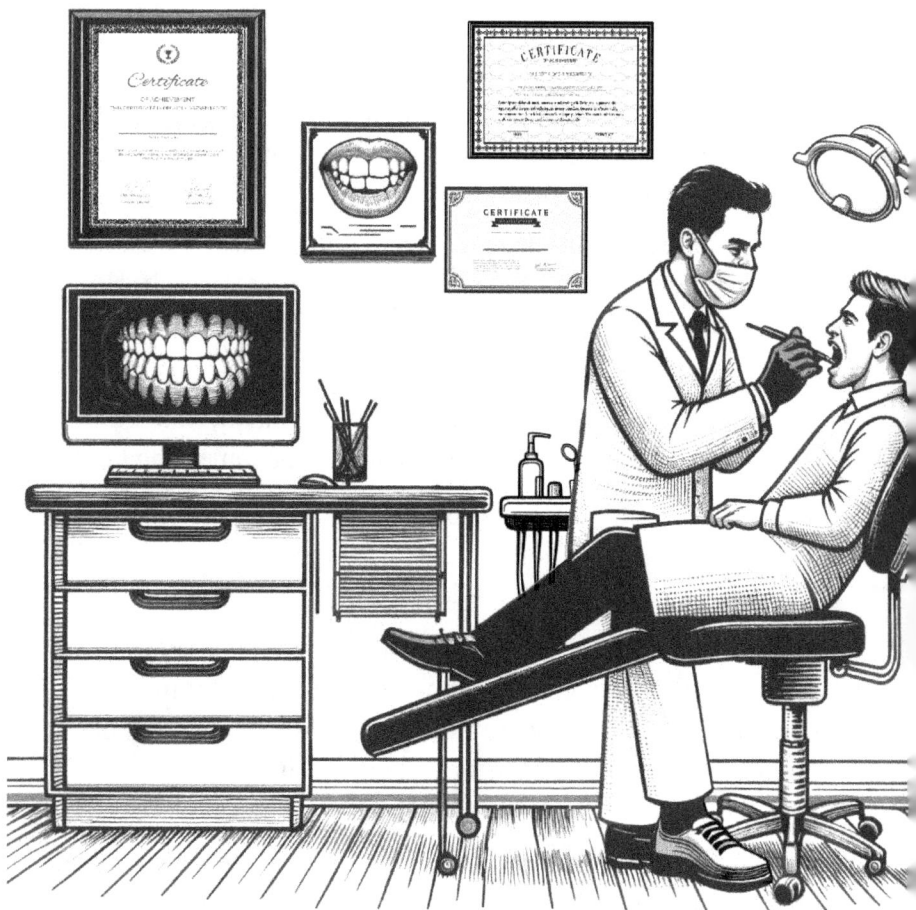

WHERE SMILES BEGIN

CHAPTER 18

Marketing Your Authority

You've built a magnetic brand that echoes with your truth and a reputation that opens doors like a master key. Now it's time to amplify your voice, not by shouting louder, but by speaking with clarity and providing value that people can't help but listen to.

Marketing your authority isn't about chasing trends or flooding feeds on forums or social media with noise. It's about showing up with purpose, solving problems with precision, and building a presence so steady it becomes undeniable.

Why Authority Matters?

Authority isn't about being the loudest person in the room; it's about being the one people trust when the stakes are high. The quiet confidence makes clients lean in, partners seek out, and the board turn to you for answers. In a world where everyone's vying for attention, authority is your edge. It makes people choose your solution over a cheaper knockoff down the street, recommend you without hesitation, and believe in your vision before you've even finished explaining it. Your actions and your work will speak for themselves.

Marketing your authority isn't about flashing ads on a billboard or something going viral. It's about showing up, hearing your audience's struggles, feeling their pain, and crafting answers that hit home. When you market with authority, you're not just selling, you're leading, solving, and building trust that may pay dividends for years, if not now in the present.

It's easy to get sucked into the whirlwind of trends churning out endless posts or jumping on every platform and mimicking others' successes. *But noise doesn't build authority; it buries it.* If you're blasting generic content or chasing clicks without substance, you will be just another voice in the crowd, whom no one will recognize. You will be just one in 7 billion people. So why will they listen to you? Authority comes from coherence, delivering value that is so clear and so consistent that people will feel that you're speaking directly to them. It's not about being everywhere; it's about being unforgettable by offering them what matters most and what counts to them.

How to Market Your Authority?

Building authority is like laying down train tracks- It must be steady, strong, deliberate, and lead you somewhere real. It's about blending heart and wisdom, showing up where your clients are, and delivering value that feels personal to them. Once you capture their heart, they will be your loyal customers for life.

Here's how to make your voice they trust:

1. Speak from the Heart, Solve with the Mind
Your marketing should do two things: solve a problem and soothe a pain. Blend sharp insights with genuine care, and you'll create content that doesn't just inform, but will resonate.

- **Mix Reflection and Utility**: Share how you think about a problem (By failing at it) and how you would solve it (by giving a step-by-step fix). An athlete might post about her burnout, and also share a quick mindfulness trick that worked for her.

- **Anticipate Their Needs**: Don't wait for your audience to express their struggles. If you're a designer, write a post like, "Struggling to make your brand pop? Here's one trick that will grab your attention." Once they grasp it, help them solve their problem before they've fully named it.

- **Be a Friend**: Converse with your client as you would with a friend over coffee. Cite your experiences and how you had overcome your difficulties. Avoid jargon or using complicated words. Keep it plain and simple. "I've been there, and here's what helped me." It builds trust faster than any polished pitch. You will need to connect with their problems and then offer your solutions.

2. Layer Quick Hits with Deep Dives

Authority grows when you meet people where they are. Some may be doubtful, while others are ready to dig in. Use short, punchy sentences to spark curiosity, then use the larger chunks to build conviction. Together, they create a rhythm that helps pull people in and keeps them committed.

- **Quick Hits for Curiosity**: Share a short tip, a question, or a story that grabs attention. For example: "3 mistakes I made pricing my services and how I fixed them." It's bite-sized but opens the door to more questions, such as " How did you do it? This sparks curiosity and inquisitiveness.

- **Deep Dives for Conviction**: Follow up with a longer piece, such as an essay or a detailed guide that shows your expertise. This may be portrayed as: "How I doubled my rates without losing clients." This may help attest to and validate you as an authority in the field.

- **Keep the Flow**: Alternate between short and long posts to help build momentum. A quick tip might hook a new client; a deep dive seals their trust. Showcase your achievements too to set your foundation.

3. Show Up Where They're Already Looking

You don't need to blanket every corner of the internet by posting everywhere. Authority comes from having a steady presence where people already gather. This is not something new.

- **Find Their Hangouts**: Are your clients swapping ideas in niche forums? Listening to podcasts? Scrolling video platforms? Go where they go, not where the noise is. Join a small business forum and answer questions. This may help you become a trusted voice.

- **Be a Fixer of Problems**: Show up consistently. Post weekly comments and do guest speeches in relevant spaces. A Chef may share weekly blogs in a local foodie group, becoming the go-to for event menus.

- **Add Value, Don't Sell**: Share insights, not sales pitches. Answer a question, share a lesson, and help solve a minor problem for free. A coach dropping a quick tip in a community chat can spark a client inquiry without ever pushing.

4. Let Your Voice Carry Intimacy

Your voice, whether in text, audio, or video, should feel like a conversation that provides warmth, not a broadcast. It's the closeness that builds authority and trust.

- **Use Audio to Connect**: A short voice note or audio clip can feel more personal than a long article. A fitness trainer might share a 30-second pep talk: "Feeling stuck? Try this one move to get unstuck." It may feel like a nudge from a friend. It may feel like a conversation between two friends.

- **Write Like You Speak**: Ditch the corporate tone. Use friendly and straightforward words you'd say to a friend. The key is to be Human. Humans have feelings, and they are social beings. A post like this may capture their attention: "I messed this up, so you don't have to. Here's the fix:" This title is captivating enough for them to lean in and listen.

- **Be You, Always**: Don't mimic someone else's style or character. Just be you. Showcase your genuine identity. How you walk, how you talk, and your way of seeing the world are what make your voice stick. Keep it real and untainted.

5. Prove Your Authority Through Action

Authority isn't claimed, it's earned. Every problem you solve, every promise you keep, and every client you help transform adds weight to your voice.

- **Show Results**: Share real outcomes without bragging. But showcase your achievements proudly. They may serve as proof of work completed. An Architect might post, "Helped a client build a home to their specifications and saved them 25% in construction costs,". The proof is in the impact it imparts.

- **Be Consistent**: Deliver value regularly, whether a weekly tip or a monthly deep dive. Consistency shows that you're not a one-hit wonder. Consistency, repetition, and discipline are the drivers.

- **Listen and Adapt**: Pay attention to what your audience responds to and what they are seeking. If a post about pricing strategies gets traction, dive deeper into that topic. Let their feedback be your guide.

Importance of building Authority in a crowded market

When you market for authority, you don't just build a following; you build a massive movement. One thoughtful post can spark a client's breakthrough. A question answered can turn a stranger into a fan. Consistent presence can make you the name people trust when they need answers. They will remember you, and you will be the go-to person for their needs. Your authority doesn't just grow your business; it helps you grow personally in the community and beyond.

Over time, your consistent value in your niche will help increase your referral base. People will come to you and not the other way around.

Things to avoid while building your Authority

Marketing your authority is powerful and tricky. Steer clear of these traps:

1. **Chasing Trends**: Don't jump too many hoops. Stick to one. Focus on where your clients are.

2. **Don't Sound Like a Robot**: Avoid stiff, generic content. Speak like you, and not what is in a textbook.

3. **Ignoring Feedback**: If your audience isn't engaging, you're not solving their problems. It's time to listen to them and act on what they have to say. Then give them what they want- solutions.

4. **Over-Promising**: Don't promise and hype what you can't deliver. Authority comes from giving results, not from beating around the bush. Get the job done.

Your First Step to Authority

The first step is to show up, listen, and help solve the problem promptly and orderly.

- **Listen**: Know where your clients are. What problem are they facing and talking about?

- **Solve**: Share one piece of content, or a quick tip that addresses their problem and helps solve it.

- **Engage**: Spend a few minutes daily connecting with your clients, answering questions, and responding to comments.

Ask Yourself: *What problem can I solve for someone today?* That answer will be the spark to cement your authority in society.

CHAPTER 19

Selling Without Being Salesy

You've crafted a magnetic brand that draws people in, a reputation that holds them close, and a voice that commands trust. Now comes the moment where trust turns into action. This is the moment you have been waiting for the sale.

Selling isn't a transaction, it's a transformation. It's about listening so deeply that you uncover needs they didn't name, understand, or know they wanted in the first place. But you told them anyway. Every conversation that you have, every problem you solve, every "yes" or "no" you handle with grace builds a business that's not just profitable but purposeful.

Selling done right isn't manipulation, it's a gift. It's the art of guiding someone from their struggle to your solution to their problem, which makes them feel seen, heard, and empowered. A smart sale doesn't just close a deal; it opens a new relationship that pays dividends through loyalty, referrals, and growth. It's not about convincing people to buy, it's about showing them how your solution can help transform their world.

The Trap of Pushy Selling

It's easy to slip into the trap of high-pressure tactics by offering flashy discounts, fake urgency, and perfectly rehearsed scripts that sound like a late-night infomercial. *Pushy selling repels more than it attracts.*

People smell an agenda from a mile away, eroding trust faster than you can rebuild it. If you're chasing the close of a sale instead of building the connection, you're not just losing sales, you're losing the heart of your business. Smart selling is about serving your customers so well that their "yes" will feel like it was their idea, not from your pressure to sell. They will own their decision and will take full responsibility for it.

Strategies to Sell Smartly

Selling without being salesy is about building trust early, listening deeply, and guiding with care. These strategies will help you turn conversations into commitments while maintaining your integrity.

Focus on building relationships, and the business will come to you. Never focus on the product, but explain the benefits of having that product to the customer and zero in on how it will make them feel. That's not pushing anything on the customer they do not want, but making them educated. A well-educated customer will trust you and know in his or her heart that you have their best interest in mind and not the mind of a salesperson.

1. Pave the Permission Path
Smart selling starts long before the ask; it begins with trust earned through value and connection.

- **Warm Them with Value**: Share free insights, a quick tip, a short story, or a useful resource before using any sales pitch. A fitness coach might post a 5-minute workout for busy parents, ending with, "Want more ways to stay fit on the go?" That's an invitation, not a shove.

- **Show Your Human Side**: Be open about your journey, your struggles, your wins, and your why. A caterer might share how they burned their first big order but learned to nail every event since. It builds relatability that primes the sale.

- **Ask for the Green Light**: Before offering your solution, ask, "Are you open to exploring how we can fix this?" or "Would you like help taking the next step?" This simple question gives them control and helps make the sale feel collaborative and not forced.

2. Craft Conversations That Uncover Truth

A sales call isn't about pushing your offer; it's about peeling back layers to reveal the real problem. Smart selling needs to listen more than it talks.

- **Ask Soul-Stirring Questions**: Go beyond "What's your goal?" "What's the toll this problem is taking on you?" "How does this struggle hit your day-to-day?" "What's it like waking up to this bottleneck every morning?" Their answer points to the heart of their true need. These are real-life problems looking for real-life answers and solutions.

- **Reflect and Connect**: Mirror their words to show you get it. If someone says, "I'm drowning in emails," you might respond, "How much time is that stealing from you?" You could offer them a solution: "What if you could cut that time in half?"

- **Guide, Don't Push**: Let their story lead the conversation. It's about their journey, and not your agenda. Guide them to what they want, and they will need to make the final choice. Your job is to offer them solutions.

3. Turn Objections into Opportunities

Objections aren't walls; they are your client's fears. Smart selling uses them to deepen the conversation, not dodge it. Know their fears and learn more about them. Ask them what they are looking for and offer them just that.

- **Reframe the Hesitation**: When they say, "It's too expensive," don't slash your price. But ask, "expensive compared to what?" or "What would make this feel like a no-brainer for you?" What are they lacking in terms of information? Are they worried about time or cost?

- **Uncover the Real Blockage**: Dig into their objection with curiosity. When they are not ready, they may say, "I'm not sure I need this right now." You may ask them, "What's holding you back from feeling ready?" Know your customer well, learn the psychology of money, and learn ways to help your clients get what they want.

- **Show the Stakes**: Help them see the cost of inaction. Ask, "What happens if this problem sticks around for another six months?" They may open up, be straightforward, and give you their answer. You should respect their decision and make it a point to follow up with them periodically, reminding them of potential consequences of not attending to the problem now and kicking the can down the road. They know all too well that the dirt will eventually surface.

4. Exit with Class, No Matter the Answer

A "no" isn't a dead end, it's a detour. How you handle rejection shapes your reputation as much as a "yes" does. Smart selling leaves every interaction stronger.

- **Stay Gracious**: If they say no, thank them: "I appreciate you taking the time to talk this through." It shows respect and keeps the connection warm. They will be in touch with you when they are ready.

- **Seek Feedback**: Ask, "What could've made this a better fit for you?" Their answer might reveal issues they are facing and are not ready yet, but will soon. They may even change their mind. The answer to when they will be ready is: it depends.

- **Leave a Gift**: Offer a small parting resource, a tip, a checklist, or a kind word of thanks can go a long way. You may say, "This might help you until you're ready." We are here for you. You can reach me anytime. It will keep the door open.

5. Solve Before the Sale

The smartest sales may not feel like sales; they feel like solutions that have been set in motion. Show your value before asking for a commitment, and the "yes" will come naturally.

Everyone likes something for FREE. When you receive something for nothing, you will develop a guilty feeling for not having given something in return. This is completely natural and instinctive. This is to be Human.

- **Give a Free Taste**: Offer a small, tangible, tailored tip, or a sample of your work. A photographer might share a free lighting tip to show their expertise before pitching a shoot.

- **Paint the Possibility**: Show them what's on the other side. Instead of saying "Buy my service," you may say, "Picture having your evenings back. What would you do with all that saved-up time?"

- **Be Their Ally**: Position yourself as a partner in their success, not as a vendor but as a trusted friend. "Let's figure out how to make this work within your budget and towards your goals."

6. Nurture the Long Game

Smart selling isn't just about getting the immediate "yes," it's about building relationships that may pay off over time.

- **Follow Up with Care**: Check in without pushing after a meeting or conversation. A quick message will help serve as a reminder.

- **Stay Visible**: Share consistent value where your clients are seen. You may send them weekly tips, real-life stories, and insights. Make sure they provide usefulness and value. Always showcase your expertise.

- **Celebrate Their Wins**: If a prospect achieves something, acknowledge it. Send them a thank you email or a small gift. It may help build goodwill that may translate to sales later.

Why do you need to sell Smartly?

When you sell by serving, you don't just win clients, you win advocates. One deep conversation can turn a prospect into a raving fan. One "no" can spark a referral months later. One solved problem can ripple into a network of trust that fuels your business. Smart selling builds more than income; it builds a legacy of impact and freedom.

Selling smartly is powerful but requires finesse. Avoid these traps:

1. **Pitching Too Early**: Don't sell before you've built trust. Always give value first.

2. **Talking Over Listening**: If you speak more than they do, you're not serving. Let them tell their story and let them lead.

3. **Fearing Rejection**: A "no" is just temporary feedback. Get over it and move on. If they need you, they will call you.

4. **Forgetting to Follow-Up**: Many sales happen after the initial conversation. So, stay connected and wait.

Your First Step to Smart Selling

You don't need a perfect script, just a heart to serve and a strategy to guide you. It's that simple.

- **Give Value**: Always provide something of value for free immediately after your first conversation.

- **Dive Deep**: In your next conversation, ask a question to uncover and understand their real struggle or what they are looking for.

- **Stay Gracious**: If a prospect says no, thank them and keep the connection warm. Value the relationship more than the sale.

Pushing will most inevitably kill a sale. Give them time and space. Do your part, step back, and wait. Listen to your customers.

Feel them by understanding their requirements. Once you build a connection, they will look up to you for advice before making any purchase. This happens only through trust.

PART 5

SCALING AND SYSTEMIZING:
Turn Your Solutions into a Thriving Empire

Chapter 20

Build a Team to Scale

You've built a magnetic brand, a rock-solid reputation, and a voice that commands trust. Your sales flow naturally, serving so deeply that clients can't help but say yes. But there's a limit to what you can do alone. You need a team to solve bigger problems and unlock the riches wealth. Not just any team, but the one that breathes life into your vision, multiplies your reach, and frees you up to focus on what you can do. Delegate and oversee.

Scaling isn't about working harder; it's about working smarter, with people who amplify your strengths and fill in your gaps. A team lets you solve more problems, serve more clients, and help create more impact without burning out. They're not just hired hands; they're your co-creators, your problem-solvers, and your champions. A great team doesn't just handle tasks; they carry your mission forward, making your business bigger, better, and freer at scale.

Without a team, you will be a bottleneck. With a team, you will be a catalyst. They help free you to strategize, innovate, and live the life of a Rich Problem Solver. Rich in time, wealth, and purpose. But building a team isn't about filling seats; it's about finding the right people who get it, who can grow it, who make it theirs, and help scale it exponentially.

It's tempting to stay a one-person show all the while. Teams may sound like a hassle: hiring, managing, payroll, and all that office drama. You might think, "I can do it faster all by myself," or "No one will care as much as I do." But that mindset will cap your growth. You'll hit a ceiling where your time, energy, and skills can't stretch further. Worse, you'll burn out, stuck in the weeds of tasks that will drain you. A team isn't a burden; it may be your bridge to freedom. The trap isn't building a team but thinking you can scale alone without one.

How to Build a Team That Helps Scale?

Building a team to scale is about finding the right people, hiring with intention, managing with clarity, and motivating with purpose. Here's how to do it deeply and deliberately:

1. Know Who You Need

Before you hire, be clear on what part of your business needs to scale. Be specific. A team isn't about cloning yourself; it's about complementing your strengths and filling in where your weaknesses lie.

- **Map Your Gaps**: List the tasks eating your time and the skills you may lack, such as bookkeeping, marketing, customer support, and tech. A business consultant might consult with you and recommend that you need a virtual assistant to handle scheduling and a content creator to amplify their voice.

- **Start Small**: Don't hire a full crew at once. Begin with one key role that frees you to focus on high-impact work. For example, a caterer might hire a logistics coordinator to manage deliveries, and let them focus on menus and clients.

- **Think Long-Term**: Hire for where you're going, based on the vision you have for your company. If you plan to scale to digital products, you might need the right help to start in the middle and fill the managerial position later.

2. Find the Right People

Hiring isn't about resumes, it's about fit. You want people who share your values, vibe with your vision and mission, and bring skills to the table that you don't have.

- **Where to Look**: Tap your network first. Ask your existing clients, colleagues in your industry, and community members for referrals. Post job listings in niche groups or forums for your ideal candidate.

- **Qualities to Prioritize**: Look for curiosity, reliability, and a self-starter. Skills can be taught; attitude can't be.

- **Red Flags to Watch**: Avoid candidates who oversell themselves, dodge questions about past work, or seem misaligned with your values. If someone's all talk and no proof, move on.

3. Hire with Intention

Hiring is like dating. You must ask the right questions to know if it's a match. Don't just check boxes; dig into their mindset, work style, and alignment with your vision.

- **Key Questions to Ask**:

"Tell me about a time you solved a problem without being asked." (Tests initiative.)

"What's a mistake you made at work and how did you fix it?" (Reveals accountability.)

"What excites you about this role?" (Shows alignment with your mission.)

"How do you handle a tight deadline when things go wrong?" (Tests resilience.)

- **Test Their Fit**:

Give them a trial project to see how they work. For example, a virtual assistant might organize a mock schedule. It's better to spend $100 on testing than $10,000 regretting.

- **Watch for Alignment**:

Do they light up talking about your mission? Are they energetic? Are they just coming in to work for a paycheck, or do they want to be part of the team to make things happen?

4. Motivate with Purpose and Respect

A motivated team doesn't just work; they thrive. Keep them inspired by tying their role to your mission and treating them like partners.

- **Connect by showing the Why**: Show how their work matters. Such as: "Your scheduling frees me to help clients transform their businesses." or "Your planning makes every event unforgettable."

- **Recognize Their Wins**: Celebrate publicly and in private. A quick praise such as this: "You nailed that client call!" in a team meeting or sending a handwritten thank-you note goes far.

- **Give Them Ownership**: Let them take the lead on projects and suggest improvements.

- **Pay Fairly, Reward Generously**: Offer competitive rates, but add bonuses for big wins, a holiday gift, a profit-sharing cut, or extra time off. It shows them that you value their impact and contribution.

5. Manage with Clarity and Freedom

A great team doesn't need micromanaging; they need clear direction and a room to shine. Manage in a way that empowers, but does not control them.

- **Set Clear Expectations**: Create simple, outcome-focused, and clear guidelines. Communicate in detail about everything upfront to avoid misunderstandings later on. Instead of "Respond and answer to all emails," you may clarify, saying, "Ensure that every client feels heard within 24 hours."

- **Use Simple Systems**: Keep tools lean. A shared calendar for deadlines, a chat app for updates, and a project board for tasks.

- **Check In, Don't Hover**: Schedule 15-minute catch-up meeting to align. Ask questions and let them lead the conversation.

- **Foster Growth**: Offer learning opportunities - a course, a conference, or allowing time to explore a new skill to help them grow and scale up the corporate ladder.

6. Watch for Pitfalls When Hiring and Managing

Building a team is powerful and tricky.

Avoid these traps:

- **Hiring Too Fast**: Don't rush to fill a role. A bad hire costs more time and money than waiting for the right one.

- **Ignoring Culture Fit**: Skills matter, but values matter more. A talented hire who doesn't vibe with your mission and vision can disrupt your team and its flow.

- **Skimping on Onboarding**: Don't toss new hires into the deep end on day one. Create a simple guide to level them up step by step.

- **Neglecting Feedback**: Ask your team regularly, "What can I do to support you?" Ignoring their needs will kill their motivation much faster.

- **Overloading Yourself**: Delegate and oversee. Trust your team to be accountable for their work.

Your First Step to Building a Team

You don't need a big budget or a corner office to start. Start with your vision and a plan.

- **Identify**: List one task or role that's holding you back. What could you delegate to free up your time?

- **Reach Out**: Ask your network for referrals. Focus on values, not just skills.

- **Test**: Interview and give a trial run. Ask, "How would you tackle this problem?" to gauge their fit.

These quotes may say it all. No man is an Island. It takes a village to raise a child. No business can run on its own. It takes a dedicated and passionate team to make it sustainable and scalable. There are many moving parts to it, and all parts must work in sync towards a common vision and goal of the company. This needs a team that works and acts like it. By working together, sparks will fly, and that's when the magic tends to happen.

THE LIFE BENEATH THE HOOD

©2025

CHAPTER 21

Systems, Processes, and Automation

You didn't come this far to stay stuck in the loop. You didn't endure all the risks and put in all that effort, just for everything to fall apart when you step away. If you aim to build wealth that grows even when you sleep, you must embrace **systems**, **processes**, and **automation**.

You must grind harder to reach the stage where your business starts working for you, and not because of you. Your business can thrive even in your absence for a few weeks, a month, or more. But be careful, just because your business can run in your absence on autopilot doesn't mean it any longer needs you. Without intentional oversight, systems tend to degrade, and people tend to relax more and work less.

Do not neglect, nor get too comfortable, when your business gets to this stage. You will need to still work in the business, but not on it. This is just the beginning. Your company will still need your insight, input, and oversight.

Why Systems Matter More Than Hustle?

A scalable, efficient, and effective system does more than save time; it amplifies your results. It increases productivity, improves performance, reduces errors, and boosts profits. Systems are how work moves faster and smarter. A well-designed system aligns and coordinates every part of your operation. It aligns the processes and the tools into a single, purpose-driven machine.

What separates a struggling entrepreneur from a thriving one isn't how hard they work, but how well their business works without them.

Building scalable systems helps manage work effectively with minimal errors while satisfying the needs of consumers.

Systems bring about consistency, efficiency, and scalability.

A system doesn't necessarily mean machinery. It may also mean how various operational aspects in your business work in tandem with your departments and how they communicate and work in unison as a team. True freedom is not achieved by doing more, but by building systems that do the work when you're not watching.

How to Build Systems, Processes, and Automation?

Creating a business that runs like clockwork requires intention, clarity, and a commitment to simplicity. Here's a deep dive into how to build systems that scale, processes that empower, and automation that liberates:

1. Map Your Business Systems

A system is the framework that your business operates, including client acquisition, service delivery, payment processing, and team management. Start by mapping to see where you can streamline from the ground up.

- **Step 1: List Your Core Functions**: Break your business into multiple buckets: marketing, sales, delivery, operations, and finances.

- **Step 2: Identify Bottlenecks**: Start by asking, "Where am I stuck, stressed, or slowing down?" Fix these gaps in the system and automate them.

214

- **Step 3: Design the Flow**: Sketch your flowchart as to how your system should function. It could start from: inquiry → response → discovery call → proposal → signed contract → sale. Keep it lean and complete.

2. Create Clear Processes

A process is the step-by-step playbook for each system that is specific, repeatable, and teachable. Good processes ensure consistency.

- **Document Every Step**: For each core function, have a clear, well-defined, and written process. For example,

  1. Client submits order.

  2. Confirm order details within 24 hours.

  3. Work assigned to the team.

  4. Product launch.

  5. Follow up for customer feedback.

- **Keep It Simple and short**: Use bullet points and checklists. A process should fit on one page.

- **Test and Refine**: Run the process yourself or with a team member. "Does this save time? Is it clear-cut? Take out the unnecessary steps.

3. Automate What Repeats

Automation takes repetitive tasks off your plate and places them in the hands of systems that have been formulated to handle those tasks, letting tech handle the grunt work. It's not about replacing humans; it's about freeing them for high-value work. Sort of, delegating the hard work to the machines and the software that runs them.

- **Identify Repeatable Tasks**: Look for tasks you repeat daily, such as sending welcome emails, scheduling calls, and generating invoices. These could be easily automated.

- **Choose Simple Tools**: Use affordable, user-friendly tools to automate. Here are a few examples:

  o Scheduling: A tool to book client calls without back-and-forth emails.

  o Email: A system to send automated welcome sequences and payment reminders.

  o Invoicing: A platform to generate and track invoices automatically.

- **Start Small**: Automate one task first. Test it to ensure it feels personal and not robotic.

- **Monitor and Adjust**: Check automation weekly to ensure it's working the way it should. You may also add a personal touch to it if you choose to.

4. Hire and Train Systems

Your team thrives when systems and processes are clear. Hire people who can follow and improve them, then train them to own their roles.

- **Hire Process-Minded People**: Look for candidates who love structure and problem-solving.

- **Train with Clarity**: Create a simple onboarding process that explains your systems and processes. This could be via a video or a checklist.

- **Empower Improvement**: Encourage your team to suggest process tweaks and what other features may be lacking.

5. Measure and Optimize

Systems and processes aren't set-and-forget once events; they need to evolve as the business grows and scales. Regularly check what's working and what's not.

- **Track Key Metrics**: For each system, pick one or two metrics to monitor. For client onboarding, it might be "time from inquiry to signed contract." For invoicing, track "days to payment."

- **Ask for Feedback**: Get input from clients and your team. A client might point to a process gap. A team member might flag a tool that's slowing them down.

- **Tweak Monthly**: Set a recurring calendar reminder to review one system and one process.

6. Avoid Common Pitfalls

Building systems and automation is powerful, but it can go wrong if you're not careful. Watch out and prevent:

- **Overcomplicating**: Don't build a 20-step process when five will do. A complex system is as bad as having no system. People will get lost and eventually will give up.

- **Automating Too Soon**: Test a process manually before automating. If it's critically broken, automation will magnify the mess.

- **Neglecting the Human Touch**: Automation should save time and not feel cold. A welcome email should still sound like you, not like a bot.

- **Ignoring Maintenance**: Systems need regular checkups. A forgotten automation might send outdated emails, hurting your reputation. It may also affect your brand.

- **Skimping on Training**: If your team doesn't understand the process from the get-go, things will fail. Invest time in clear onboarding and maintenance training.

Systems Are Decisions Made Once

Every great system is simply a decision you no longer have to modify every day.

- Instead of asking "What do I do with new clients?" → you have an automated onboarding workflow. You have it lined up in your system.

- Instead of wondering, "Did I send the invoice?" → you use a recurring billing tool.

Imagine you're running a trucking business. You spend your mornings on logistics, warehousing, and payroll, and your evenings on sending out invoices. When you fall sick or go on a vacation, the entire business will grind to a halt without a system in place.

In this case, what do you do?

- o You create a logistics checklist for the staff

- o Have managers orchestrate the workflow

- o Coordinate departments to work together

- o Have them follow the systems and processes you have set for the company

- o You automate invoices using invoice apps

As a result, you can take your time off with less stress and have a business that is running smoothly without you in it while you are away. Without a system, you will need to be working on the job by having your physical presence onsite.

Systems aren't meant to break you. They don't weigh you down. They help lighten the load. They create space and time for thinking, growing, and leading, because you have built an engine that sustains and works itself on your behalf.

5 Core Systems Every Business Should Build and Have

1. Lead Generation Systems

Attract new customers consistently without chasing them.

Components:

- Landing page + irresistible lead magnet
- Email sequences to nurture new leads
- Scheduled, automated social content
- Optional Retargeting ads

2. Sales & Onboarding Systems

Turn leads into paying customers and onboard them seamlessly.

Components:

- Clear sales page and pricing guide
- Payment processor
- Automatic welcome emails
- Client intake forms and onboarding checklists

3. Delivery Systems

Deliver your service or product efficiently and consistently.

Components:

- SOPs (Standard Operating Procedures) for delivery tasks
- Onboarding documents and client guides

- Automated file sharing or access
- Templates for emails and updates

4. Financial Systems

Track income, expenses, and profitability with clarity and control.

Components:

- Automated invoicing and receipts
- Recurring payment setup
- Expense and income tracking dashboard
- Monthly financial reports

5. Team & Communication Systems

Manage team tasks, performance, and internal communication.

Components:

- Task management tool
- Weekly check-ins and updates
- SOP database and knowledge base

Start Small. Systemize Repetition.

You don't need expensive software or a large team to start. Begin with what you have. Document what you do repeatedly.

Ask yourself:

- What tasks do I repeat every day and every week?
- Which parts of my business tend to lose their grip when I'm away?
- Where am I wasting time or losing money due to disorganization?

If you perform a task more than twice, systematize it.

Note the steps. Create a checklist. Automate it. Most importantly, build the system so others can follow easily.

Systems don't replace people; they free people. They let you focus on growth, vision, innovation, and not just survival.

Systems are what transform your business from a daily grind into an asset. It is not something you *work in*, but something that works for you, even while you are away, 12,000 miles away.

Don't confuse motion for momentum. Don't confuse hustle for progress.

The most powerful entrepreneurs aren't the busiest. They're the most structured. They have set up systems to work for them around the clock, no matter where they are or whatever they are doing. That is how money is made, and not by trading time for money.

You don't need to do more. You will need to systematize what works and let that system do the hard work for you while you are traveling or sleeping.

CHAPTER 22

Strategic Alliances and Partnerships

You've built something powerful, a solution that adequately solves societal problems and a vision that matters. But scaling it alone is exhausting and slow. At some point, doing it all alone stops being noble and starts being naive.

There's a faster way to grow than to continue to grind in isolation. It's not another 14-hour day's work. It's not launching 10 new products. It's not running bigger, brighter ads. It's aligning yourself with the right people, because the next level isn't built alone. It's built together. You will need to put together partnerships and alliances.

If you want to grow faster, use fewer resources, minimize expenses, and get better results, you must master the art of strategic partnership.

The Smart Shortcut to Scale

Partnerships give you distribution without debt and the reach without the ads. You don't need to build an audience; you have every tool and every product. When you partner strategically, you don't just double resources, you multiply them.

You need:

- Someone who already has what you don't (Think: audience, tools, expertise)
- A shared vision or complementary purpose

- And a valuable solution worth sharing (a win-win proposition)

You don't need to:

- Build every tool
- Create every offer
- Own every relationship

You gain:

- Reach without running ads
- Credibility without lengthy introductions
- Distribution without debt

Strategic alliances are the leverage points of businesses. While small businesses burn themselves out trying to "go viral" in a crowded space, innovative founders build alliances that outlast the algorithm. In due course, they may even buy out those small businesses. Big fish eat the small fish. Why build an audience from scratch when someone else already has your ideal customer and is happy to collaborate with you?

That's how much simpler it gets.

Types of Partnerships That Help You Grow Fast

Strategic alliances aren't reserved for big companies with legal departments and boardrooms. They are for creators, solopreneurs, agencies, freelancers, tech founders, etc. Anyone with a value to offer and a craving for exponential growth. You can customize and make it practical:

1. Affiliate Partnerships

Let others promote your product for you. Then, you pay them a small commission when they generate a sale. This is purely commission-based, hence you have nothing to lose. It works

223

so that they only get paid when you get paid. It enables you to eventually expand using someone else's trust, networking, and marketing abilities to make a sale.

This partnership is great for membership sites, digital courses, software tools, and downloadable templates. To maximize outreach, you can create emails, graphics, etc., to make it easier for affiliates to promote your work.

2. Strategic Product Bundles

Combine your product or service with another brand, solving a related problem. It's important to note that the brands should not compete. For example, you can collaborate with a fitness coach, a meal planning app, a web designer, and a copywriter.

Customers love bundled value. You both win by creating a complete solution while reaching out to each other's customers. You can even try running it into a limited-time campaign to create urgency.

3. Co-Hosted Events or Content

Both parties share a platform, double the value, then split the promotion expenses and profits. You can host a live webinar with a partner, launch a challenge together, run multiple podcast series, and create a free eBook or toolkit featuring both brands.

With this, you provide more value to customers, reach new eyes, and build relationships to foster growth. You should also follow up after the event with a joint offer or bundle to convert attention into revenue.

4. Licensing and White-Labelling

You can further your reach by letting people use your framework, methodology, or product for a fee. It expands your product's impact without increasing your workload. It turns your intellectual property into passive income. Use licensing agreements to protect your brand while creating precise and legally structured terms of use.

The Power of Borrowed Trust

People don't just buy from strangers; they buy from people they trust or people trusted by people they trust. When you partner with someone your ideal customers already follow, you inherit their credibility. Their audience listens and sees you as credible because *your name was introduced by someone they already trust.*

This is called borrowed trust, and it's one of the fastest ways to leapfrog into new markets, communities, opportunities, etc., especially if your product is good but has low visibility.

At this point, you're not starting from zero; you're entering through the front door.

Choosing the Right Partner

Not all partnerships are good partnerships. Some waste time, dilute your message, or damage your reputation. Choose wisely.

Here's a quick filter to use:

- **Shared Values:** Are you aligned in ethics, mission, and voice?

- **Complementary Strengths:** Do you fill gaps in each other's offering?

- **Audience Overlap:** Do your customers benefit from knowing each other?

- **Clear a Win-Win:** Are both sides gaining real value for the audience, revenue, and in positioning?

If the answer to all four is "yes," that may be a green light. But you will need to read the fine print and jump the legal hoops before committing by doing your due diligence, etc.

If even one feels off, pause. Retrace your steps. If need be, realign with your potential partner and discuss.

What to Consider When Proposing a Strategic Partnership?

When reaching out, don't just say, "Let's collaborate." Be specific. Make it valuable. Make it easy for them to say yes. A good outreach message may include:

1. Who are you?
2. Why do you admire their work?
3. What value do you bring to them?
4. What are you proposing (clearly and briefly)?
5. What are the next steps?

Start Small, Then Scale Up

Don't wait to find the "perfect" partner or build a massive campaign. Begin with:

- A joint Live
- A co-written blog post
- A guest spot on a podcast
- A referral exchange

Small collaborations build trust. And trust leads to bigger partnerships. Take it slow and be wary.

Strategic partnerships are not just about growth, they're about acceleration. You can go alone and move fast. But with the right partner, you can go further, faster, with less stress and create a bigger impact. In the new economy, relationships are currency. Leverage them.

You don't have to own the crowd. Just find the person who does and brings something valuable to the table.

THE BILLIONAIRES' PALATE

CHAPTER 23

From Solopreneur to Scalable Enterprise

You started with drive, passion, and discipline. You took on every role and wore every hat to succeed. You practiced everything you learnt. You answered every email, made every call, and responded to every comment. You handled every decision, from the logo, invoices, customer complaints and feedback, and product delivery. Anything and Everything until now.

You started with hustle and stuck with it despite the trials and tribulations. You sold. You shipped. You survived. But there's a ceiling to hustling. Time will run out eventually, and when it does, you will find yourself stuck and unable to meet deadlines. The same customers who once were impressed by your unwavering dedication and productivity are now getting frustrated due to missed deadlines and inconsistent service outcomes. Burnout is fast approaching. Things are falling apart. Growth? *Sigh.*

Now is the time to scale.

This is your launch pad. You have your permission. Your blueprint to scale. Your guide to building something great and becoming even greater. Now, you are doing it for you and no one else.

The One-Man Business Trap

Everything worked out perfectly from the onset. You did everything, you wore all the hats. It felt good; it worked just fine. "No need to hire yet", "I can do this... this too", "I can cut this to save on expenses". Slowly, but surely, that efficiency becomes a limitation. *A beautiful trap.* You became the product. The process. The system. The whole business. A little distraction, sickness, or sudden change in mood, i.e., you feel overwhelmed, makes everything you've worked for fall into ruin. Ask yourself this: If "I took 2 weeks off... What will happen to my business?"

Being a solopreneur is not the ultimate goal; it's a suitable starting point when you initially launch your business and run it for a few years. The *Real power lies beyond the solo grind.*

The 3 Stages of Your Business Journey

1. Freelancer or Solopreneur

This puts you in the "I'm the business" point of view. You are in the driver's seat. You are an amateur who wants to do everything by yourself. You want to be the marketer, accountant, CEO, COO, the plumber, the electrician, the IT, and the customer support. The joy of flexible working hours and 100% net profit is unmatched. You keep grinding away, saying: *I'll work harder and grow faster-* with this mindset. Then comes burnout, inconsistent income, and having no time to think big, as you are trying to maintain what's left of your energy and business.

The only way out of this is to build systems and get help, figuring out a way to buy back your time.

2. Entrepreneur

By default, at this point, you take on the role of *building the business*. You've started hiring, building systems, and experimenting to know what works and doesn't in your business. You transitioned from doing everything yourself to building systems that work for you in your absence. You discover that growth comes from design, systems, and not just from efforts.

Even with everything in place, setbacks. Your mindset struggles. You fall into the trap of hiring without clearly defined roles. You start making mistakes. Then you start thinking: *It will be faster if I do it myself.* The reality is, at times, you don't always need more hands; you need better systems. Set the desired outcome you want to achieve, and communicate it with other staff. Get everyone on board with your vision for your company. Give team members full ownership of a process. Don't just assign a task; assign it to get results.

3. Enterprise Owner

The business runs, and you lead.

Your team is solid, and your systems are functional and efficient. You aren't completely involved in the day-to-day activities of your business, but it runs smoothly and efficiently. You are very much the owner. Everything runs how you want it to. You have now built an asset. It's time to stop operating and focus more on innovating and having a structure. Your leadership skills and strategic planning come into play. Step back a little, and observe. What will happen if you don't manage anything for a few days? If anything breaks, who is to be held accountable? Do you have a strategy and a backup? Do you have redundant systems in case all fail? You might re-strategize and rewire the systems to fix the problem.

At this stage, you will have systems, processes, manpower, backup systems, and management to handle anything wrong.

The Core Shift: Operator to Architect

Most people stay stuck doing the same repetitive tasks instead of redesigning. They are buried and too busy doing the to-dos instead of building what can run without them. This needs a significant shift in mindset.

You need to be no longer the doer, but the designer. You need to design roles, systems, and outcomes. It's not about getting things done; it's building a structure that gets it done for you. Be the architect of your own business. Never get too comfortable staying within the status quo and your comfort zone. Focus on doing, have a creative mindset to build something functional, long-lasting, and high-quality.

Your job isn't just to work in the business. It's to build the business and work on it. There's a big difference there.

Hire, Delegate, Empower

Hire people for outcomes, not just to complete tasks. Train them well. Give them responsibility and hold them accountable for it. Let them carve out their part. Every task you delegate should help you buy back time.

Be specific in what you want done. Instead of saying "I need someone to post two blogs weekly on social media platforms," You can modify it by saying "I need someone to grow our company engagement by 20%."

Now you can see the difference.

Build the ideal team that frees you from burnout, excessive workload, and instability. It's about having the freedom by not micromanaging. Your team should be able to work and progress without you. You've created a scalable asset by doing your part and achieving this milestone. Moving forward, you must oversee and focus on getting your desired results.

Build Assets, Not Just Income

Products, systems, and intellectual property are your legacy. Your way of helping humanity. They don't get tired. They don't get sick. They don't quit.

Create them once and monetize forever. If you build right, you get to stop working for money, and your business starts working for you.

Adopt the act of thinking like a CEO by not having an employee mindset. Ask yourself:

- If I took two weeks off, would things still run?
- Are there systems in place for delivery and quality control?
- Is my business something I do, or something I own?

If the answer to all three is "no," it's time to restructure.

Remember: You don't need to become a massive corporation. You need to become a well-structured, outcome-driven, well-oiled operation to operate around the clock. A money machine. One that works even when you don't. The best enterprises aren't the busiest; they are the most structured.

233

CHAPTER 24

Exit and Expansion

Many entrepreneurs dream of such freedom, but very few achieve it in the long run. Entrepreneurs often trap themselves in their business. Why? Because it's almost impossible for them to let go. The enterprise is their 'baby'. They can never let it grow without their constant guidance. They fail to understand that even a baby will eventually become an adult. There comes a time when you have to let that *baby* grow and thrive on its own. You can offer leadership and guidance, but only when necessary.

So, to expand and grow your enterprise, it needs to shift from operator to asset builder.

Why Exit Matters?

Exit doesn't mean leaving your enterprise entirely. It means replacing yourself in day-to-day operations. It also means:

- Hiring a Chief Operating Officer (COO)
- Licensing your intellectual property (IP)
- Automating key workflows
- Franchising your model
- Having a manager to oversee operations and report to you

You didn't come this far to remain a glorified employee of your creation. You have poured in your sweat, blood, sacrifices, and tears into your baby, and it's time for you to live your life a bit.

A proper exit ensures a well-deserved freedom, clarity, a break from the long work hours, and emotional breakdown from doing everything else alone.

How to Make Your Business Expandable or Exitable?

Systematizing everything cannot be overemphasized. As much as it has been repeated in this book, many still fail to create a structured system. As a result, when things start to wane, it becomes difficult to control the damage.

Another factor to factor into is tracking performance. It's necessary to track your enterprise's performance with real-time metrics. Know your numbers: margins, churn rate, Customer Acquisition Cost (CAC), Customer Lifetime Value (LTV), and profits per product line. Facts don't lie. Figure out what lacks and what is still in progress. You can make informed decisions when you know what's working and what's not.

Continuously develop your asset. Taking your hands off the steering wheel is not enough because your business is doing well. Your enterprise can be profitable, but will need to be self-sustaining. Your role should shift from *doing* the work personally to *growing* the company. You will also need to use the systems you have implemented to guide the business without suffocating it. Let the systems and people you've trained thrive under your vision and oversight, not in your presence.

It's yours for a reason; it requires your guidance and nurturing to thrive.

235

Leveraging Equity, Intellectual Property (IP), and Capital

"True wealth isn't earned, it's multiplied. And the keys to multiplication are equity, ownership, and leverage."

There's a concrete and vast difference between trading time for money and owning valuable business or property. Here is an analogy to compare the two:

Working for money is like fetching water from a well each day for others, for the next 60 years, whereas equity and ownership are analogous to owning the well and the water in it.

See the difference? That's night and day.

Most people chase sales revenue and cash flow. But just a handful know that wealth is built by building equity, owning Intellectual Property, having access to capital, and eventually owning and holding assets forever.

Leveraging Equity

Equity means Ownership. Both are tied to each other.

Owning your company is equity. It is also an asset on your balance sheet. You can only leverage equity if you own it and what it's worth in the free market. You can offer equity to investors to raise capital for your enterprise, but the equity in your company must be enticing enough before it can be leveraged.

How do you achieve this?

1. **Build it.** Invest in strong systems, branding, and in your products and services. Make your business valuable over time without your presence. That speaks volumes in terms of its worth.

236

2. **Protect it.** Register your business, document ownership, and secure trademarks. Keep control over your share.

3. **Grow it.** Reinvest profits. Retain equity when bringing in investors. Be the majority owner. Don't trade ownership for short-term money. Focus on your long-term goals and vision.

Investors are always on the lookout for high-value equity in highly profitable companies to invest in. Your job is to make your company attractive, priceless, and field-proven, worth every dollar they invest.

Leveraging Intellectual Property (IP)

Intellectual Property is your business's silent powerhouse. It's the knowledge, creativity, and value you've built that no one else can copy or steal.

Your IP could be:

- A signature framework and custom methodology
- Your course content, digital products, and proprietary apps
- Your logo, slogan, and brand design
- Proprietary software, processes, and databases

The key is to *recognize* that your ideas are valuable, then take the steps to protect and package them legally.

Here's how to leverage IP:

1. **Protect it legally.** Trademark your brand. Copyright your content. Patent your inventions.

2. **Productize it.** Turn your ideas into scalable products: Build toolkits, write ebooks, conduct workshops, and offer subscriptions.

237

3. **License it.** Allow others to use your framework or tool for a fee. This is how IP creates passive income, which is steady and predictable.

"Don't just teach your ideas, own them."

When someone else uses your content, strategy, or creation, you should benefit from that usage. That's the power of intellectual property. It earns for you even when it's hands off.

Leveraging Capital

Capital is fuel, and it helps accelerate everything. That is, *if* you have it and are ready for it. But capital isn't just money. It may also encompass trust. No one will fund chaos, but will fund clarity, control, and capability.

There are three ways to access capital:

1. **Personal capital:** your savings and profits reinvested

2. **Debt capital:** loans, lines of credit, and revenue-based financing

3. **Equity capital**: funding from investors in exchange for a percentage of the company

How to become fundable?

- **Know your numbers:** P&L, projections, growth trends

- **Build trust:** clean branding, solid operations, customer growth

- **Have a plan:** show them how your company's growth will help them increase their equity position, profit margin, and their investment in your company.

"People don't invest in ideas; they invest in execution." They like to see results.

Use capital strategically to grow your systems, amplify your most compelling offer, and expand into new markets. Don't just use it to patch short-term issues but build scalable solutions that endure. When you do, opportunities will help you solve even bigger problems.

PART 6

HAVING THE MINDSET OF A RICH PROBLEM SOLVER
Develop the Mindset That Turns Complex Problems into Profitable Solutions

CHAPTER 25

Mental Models
of Millionaire Thinkers

Most people don't stay broke because they're lazy. They stay broke because they've been taught to think about money incorrectly.

I know, because I used to think that way too. Growing up, I was fed the same tired script: go to school, get a good job, save a little each month, and maybe, *maybe* I'll retire comfortably. It all sounded safe back then, but now I understand it was a trap. That was before the Internet era.

There was no such thing as the Internet. You go to a library and read books, hoping and praying that the book you want is available. That mindset kept me stuck, chasing short-term fixes and shiny distractions instead of building real wealth. It wasn't until I started studying the mental models of millionaire thinkers on the internet in the later years that I realized that the game was rigged, not by some shadowy elite, but by my thinking.

Here's the truth: Creating wealth isn't just about earning and spending less. It's about rewiring your brain, rethinking your thought process about money, time, and opportunity. Millionaires don't just work harder; they think differently. They use mental models frameworks for making decisions, which let them see opportunities where others see obstacles.

You will need to think differently and be different to get extraordinary results. If not, you will be just another fish in the pond.

Below are four mental models that transformed how I approach wealth: Long-Term Thinking, First Principles, Asymmetric Bets, and Building Long-Term Wealth.

Long-Term Thinking: Play the Infinite Game

Most people are obsessed with quick wins, playing lottery tickets, falling for get-rich-quick schemes, and looking for that one stock tip from a friend's cousin that can make them rich. Millionaires, on the other hand, play the long game. They understand that wealth isn't built in a day, a month, or a year. It may take decades. It's built through consistent, deliberate actions compounded over time. It sounds simple, and it is. But who is willing to wait these days?

When they are broke, most people would blow their entire paycheck on things that feel good in the moment, gambling, lottery, a fancy, well-deserved vacation, a new phone they don't need but want. To get their mind away from the problem, they may succumb to and pick up habits such as smoking, drinking, and gambling, to name a few. They are trading their future for instant gratification. Millionaires do the opposite. They ask, "How will this decision impact me in 5, 10, or 20 years?" Hence, they have a long-term time horizon and invest in appreciating assets such as stocks, real estate, and skills that grow over time. They do not throw money at liabilities that depreciate when you buy them. They focus on building assets that will, in due course, pay for their liabilities. This helps them preserve their capital to generate income.

It's not about deprivation but prioritizing future freedom over current status. That also prioritizes delayed gratification through discipline. Adopting a long-term thinking mindset means you must stop asking, "What can I buy now?" and ask, "What will this capital help me build now that will help me 5 years from now?". That is planning, capital preservation, and investing at its best.

First Principles: Break It Down to the Core

The first principle is to reason everything from the ground up, questioning everything until you hit undeniable truths. Most people will accept rules and the status quo at face value: "You need a college degree to succeed," or "You can't start a business without a big loan." Millionaires don't fall for all this. They strip away assumptions and rebuild their understanding from scratch. They create their own rules by writing them. Then they follow those rules and principles to help guide them in wealth creation.

I used to think I needed a "stable" job to make money, and this was the only way - by trading my time for dollars. This is what I was taught from a young age. My dad did the same and worked a 9-5 job until he retired. When I broke them down and learned from them as I grew, I noticed that this job had a capped income.

I also understood that I could scale indefinitely without trading time for money if I had my own business or had partnerships and stakes in other companies.

This mental model forces you to question everything. Why rent when you could buy a multi-family home and have tenants cover the mortgage and expenses? Why save in a bank account that is losing value to inflation when you could invest in other asset classes that bring in much higher returns? First principles thinking isn't just about money, it's about refusing to accept "that's just how it's done" as an answer.

Asymmetric Bets: Small Risks, Big Rewards

Millionaires don't gamble; they make calculated bets where the downside is small, with a massive upside. These are asymmetric bets. Most people avoid risks altogether. Millionaire thinkers seek opportunities where the potential reward far outweighs the risk and the cost. Their decisions are well-calculated based on years of experience, expertise, knowledge, and wisdom.

Always make it a point to invest in yourself. This gives you the biggest return on Investment (ROI). Asymmetric bets don't always make money.

You will be losing money, time, or effort in each endeavor. Spending 10 hours learning about money management could net you $100,000 in your financial portfolio. That's a great ROI for the time and effort taken. The key is to look for opportunities where the downside is limited, but the upside is uncapped. Millionaires are always hunting for these. Make sure to look for opportunities with uncapped income potential. For example, a sales job could give you that. But here you are again, trading time for money. Find ways to make money passively after you put in your initial and upfront work. This may include capital, too.

Building Long-Term Wealth: Systems Over Goals

Goals are overrated. "I want to be a millionaire" sounds nice, but it's just a finish line. Where are the steps to get there? Millionaires focus on systems—repeatable processes that stack the odds in their favor. Your goal might be to save $10,000 a month, but a system can help automate your investments, diversify your income streams, and upskill you to increase your earning power. That's when you will have a system that works for you.

When I started creating financial systems for myself, my life changed dramatically. I set it up once, and then I forgot about it. It was working for me behind the scenes in the darkness and silence. I set up automatic transfers to an investment account before I could spend my paycheck and created a side hustle that generated passive income. I committed to reading one book a week on business or finance.

The beauty of systems is that they don't rely on willpower or need you to be available. You set them up once, and they run. Millionaires know that wealth isn't about one big win—it's about creating a machine that churns out value year after year with little to no effort on their part.

The Power of Leverage: Amplify Your Efforts

Another mental model millionaire thinkers use is leverage. They don't just trade time for money; they find ways to make their time, money, and resources work harder for them by allocating them appropriately. Leverage is about amplifying your impact without proportionally increasing your effort. Think of it like using a lever to lift a heavy object: a little force on one end creates a big result on the other side.

When I was stuck in my old mindset, I thought working more hours was the only way to earn more money. But millionaires use leverage to break that equation. They might hire a team to scale their business, use technology to automate tasks, and invest in assets that generate income without further input. For instance, by creating an online course, you build leverage, creating it once, and it can sell thousands of times. You do the work upfront and wait to capitalize on it later. Compare that to a job where you're paid only for your work hours.

That's leverage: one effort, multiple payoffs. Millionaires always ask, "How can I make this effort produce exponential results?". So they are very calculative about where they park their money. When parked, that money has to work for them. The middle class and the poor work differently: They work, pay their bills, spend and invest the rest, if anything else remains. They spend money on liabilities and live off credit. Hence, the cycle repeats; Monday arrives, they go to work, spend, spend, and the cycle continues. The millionaires invest, wait, and then reap the benefits. They have practiced patience and learned to wait for the right time.

Scarcity vs. Abundance: Choose Your Lens

The final mental model is about the shift from a scarcity mindset to an abundance mindset. Most people operate from scarcity, hoarding resources and fearing that there's not enough. "If I invest this $150,000 into a business, I might lose it." Fear keeps them away.

Millionaires see the world through a different lens-abundance. They believe opportunities are everywhere, and money can be made by repeating the process multiple times.

This hit home when I hesitated to invest in a course that could've boosted my skills. I was scared of "losing" the money because what little I had, I was afraid to lose. That was in the late 80s. A millionaire thinker would've seen it as an investment in future earnings. Back then, I did not know better. I was aware of few to no books on finance then, and people I knew back then never talked about money. Abundance thinking means you're not afraid to take risks because you trust you can recover and create more. It's why millionaires negotiate harder, start businesses, and invest aggressively.

They usually position themselves as investment-rich and cash-poor.

Shifting to an abundance mindset changed how we see competition. Instead of envying someone's success, we can learn from what they have done: "How can I learn from them?" or "How can we collaborate?" and make it a big win for both parties. By combining the strengths, we can tap into each other's attributes, achievements, network, and knowledge. It's a simple shift, but it helps open doors we didn't even know existed.

Rewire Your Mind, Rewrite Your Future

These mental models, Long-Term Thinking, First Principles, Asymmetric Bets, Building Long-Term Wealth, Leverage, and Abundance Mindset, aren't just available to millionaires. They're tools anyone can use.

The difference between being broke and being wealthy isn't luck or talent. It's a mindset. Start thinking like a millionaire, and you'll see opportunities you never noticed. The question is: Are you ready to change by reframing and changing your thinking?

FROM SERVICE TO SIGNIFICANCE

©2025

CHAPTER 26

Resilience in the Face of Rejection

Rejection stings. Whether it's a "no" from a potential client, a failed business pitch, or the crushing silence of "no one cares,". It feels personal. You may have poured your heart into a project, only to have it ignored or shot down. Early on, I thought rejection meant I wasn't good enough. But over time, I learned that rejection isn't a verdict on your worth; it's a test of your resilience.

I also realized that it *takes many No's to get a Yes.*

The most successful people in the world aren't the ones who avoid failure; they're the ones who keep going despite it. They fall and get up. They have fallen on multiple occasions. But they still keep moving forward. Learn to accept failure and never take "no" for an answer. Persist and persevere in the face of rejection. Be consistent and be disciplined. Keep pushing yourself. *Remember that*: *If anything were that easy, everyone would do it.* If you want it bad enough, you must push yourself with all you've got.

Resilience isn't about ignoring the pain of rejection or pretending it doesn't hurt. It's about reframing failure, building mental toughness, and turning "no" into a stepping stone. Here's how to handle the sting of "no one cares,". Deal with rejection, get used to it, and bounce back from many more rejections and failures stronger than before. You will come out much stronger on the other side.

Handling "No One Cares"

There's nothing more demoralizing than pouring your energy, heart, and soul into a project, a business idea, or a job application- only to be met with indifference. That will take you down if you are not prepared mentally.

Here's what I have learned over the years: "no one cares" isn't about you; it's about timing, audience, or execution. People are busy, distracted, or unprepared for what you're offering. Instead of taking it personally, step back and analyze. Did you reach the right people? Was your message clear? Millionaires don't sulk when they hear silence they tweak their approach and rewrite the script after their first misstep or mislaunch. They may rewrite their investment pitch, target a different audience, and relaunch under different branding. This time, it will sell because they have learned a lot about the approach, methods, and path.

The key is to treat indifference as feedback, not failure. Ask yourself: What can I adjust? Can I clarify my value? Can I find a better platform? Resilience means you don't let silence stop you; you let it guide you to have a better strategy by creating your pathway.

Dealing with Rejection

Rejection is a universal experience, but it hits harder, especially when you dream big. Get used to this common response: "Thanks, but we're not interested." thinking, where did you go wrong, or what was their expectation of your product or service? Was it the price issue? What did they not like about your product? How can you improve it in the 2.0 version?

Here's what separates the resilient from the defeated: rejection isn't the end of the road; it's only a detour and a temporary one. That should fire you up by accepting it as a challenge to do much better the next time around.

Millionaires don't see "no" as a stop sign; they see it as a chance to refine their approach or find a new path. Rejection is just part of the process. Rejection happens every day in your life, too. You don't cry over spilled milk. You clean it, accept it, and move on.

When you face rejection, do these three things: First, feel the sting. It's okay to be disappointed. Second, analyze and accept the "no." What was wrong with the pitch? Was your timing right? Or maybe it was not a fit for them? Third, act and move on. That is not the ned of the line. There are many more clients out there waiting for your services. Reach out to someone new, improve your offer, and pivot entirely. Every "no" brings you closer to a "yes" if you keep moving and being consistent in your efforts.

Learning from Failures

Failure feels like hitting a brick wall, but it's an excellent teacher in disguise. Failure teaches you more about business than any book or course ever could. You will learn to vet partners better, test ideas before going all in, and to cut your losses early. You will also be wary and alert. All these attributes you pick up along the way come from real-life experience.

Millionaires don't fear failure—they embrace it. It gives them valuable data. Each flop reveals to you what doesn't work, and helps sharpen your instincts. Resilience means treating every failure as a lesson, not a defeat. You must fail multiple times to succeed in anything you do. *Most importantly, you must get it right only once to make it big.*

251

To learn from failure, ask: What went wrong? What can I control next time? What can I improve? What other skills do I need ot learn? Write them down, make a plan, and move forward. Don't lament over your failures and get stuck in one spot. The faster you extract the lesson, the sooner you can pivot to something better. Maybe it was not for you.

Building Mental Toughness

Resilience isn't just about bouncing back; it's about building a mindset to take the hits and keep going. Most people crumble under criticism and setbacks. They take it personally. They need to understand that it is part of the game. Mental toughness comes from practice, not magic. Here's how to build it:

- **Reframe the Narrative**: Instead of "I failed," think, "I found a way that didn't work." Instead of thinking "They don't care," think differently: "I haven't found my right customer yet." Your words shape your reality. Same problem, different results.

- **Focus on What You Can Control**: You can't control whether someone buys your product or loves your idea, but you can control your effort, preparation, and response. Focus there.

- **Celebrate Small Wins**: Rejection and failure can make you feel stuck. Counter it by tracking progress, no matter how small. Did you make one more call today? Learn one new skill? That's a win in itself.

- **Surround Yourself with Supporters**: Find people who help lift you, mentors, trusted friends, and even trusted family. Sometimes, online communities may give you a hand. They'll all remind you that setbacks are temporary.

Turning Rejection into Fuel

The most successful people don't avoid rejection; they use it. Every "no" is a chance to grow, refine, and get closer to your goal. I used to dread pitching ideas, terrified of being turned down. Now, I see each rejection as a badge of courage. It makes me stronger and fired up. It is your space, and you have control over it. You need to decide on how you will accept rejection.

Resilience isn't about being unbreakable; it's about bending without breaking. It's about hearing "no one cares" and responding, "I'll take that as a challenge and turn the ship around." It's about facing rejection and saying, "Next." And it's about failing, learning, and coming back much stronger. The path to success is paved with a lot of "Nos". But keep walking, and you'll meet someone who will give you their "Yes". Then you will have accomplished what you have been looking for all along.

CHAPTER 27

Discipline Over Dreams

Dreams are seductive. They're the spark that gets you out of bed each morning. It may be the vision of a better life, a thriving business, or having financial freedom to do whatever you want on your terms. But dreams alone don't pay the bills. I learned this the hard way when I spent months fantasizing about a "perfect" business idea, only to watch it fizzle and disappear because I didn't consistently work to make it real. Dreams are easy; discipline is hard. And discipline is what turns ideas into results. You may have the best invention, but it will be gone if you don't churn your idea and execute on time. It will be gobbled up by somebody else. It will be one of those missed opportunities, and it comes at a cost- your opportunity cost.

Most people chase the wrong thing. They obsess over the product, their shiny app, viral book, and a potential million-dollar startup, and wait until it is perfected, hoping it'll be their ticket to wealth.

But millionaires know better. They focus on solving real problems, trusting that the money will follow. Discipline and consistency, not dreaming, are what build empires. Here's how to prioritize discipline over dreams and obsess over the problem, not the product.

The Trap of Chasing Dreams

I used to think success was about having the best idea. I'd spend hours sketching out logos for my business, imagining my brand on billboards, or picturing myself on a podcast talking about my product. But when it came time to execute, I'd stall. I'd tweak the design, rewrite the plan, or wait for the "perfect" moment and await perfection. Waiting for perfection pushed me back each day.

Sounds familiar? That's the dream trap, getting lost in the fantasy of success without working to get there. Also, perfection does not exist. Just complete it to what you feel is right, get it out there, and monitor consumer feedback. Then tweak it and re-release as the next edition. That's why we have different versions of the first. 2.0, 3.0, 4.0, etc. This may not be because the first edition was bad, but the subsequent versions may have been polished and presented well with additional information.

Dreams feel good, but they're fleeting. They make you feel productive without actually moving the needle. Millionaires don't fall for this. They know that success isn't about bringing to market the prettiest product or the flashiest pitch it's about solving a problem people care about. And solving problems takes discipline: the grit to show up every day, even when the dream feels far away.

Obsess Over the Problem

My biggest mistake early on was falling in love with my product. I built a website for a niche I thought was cool, but I didn't ask if anyone needed it. Spoiler: they didn't. I wasted months because I was obsessed with my creation and did not focus on the problem it was supposed to solve. Even if the need was there, would people embrace change from their current habits and be willing to accept my product? I was not so sure. This is where market research and marketing come in, for which I did not have the funds.

Millionaires flip this script. They start with the problem. They ask, "What pain are people feeling? What do they need that they're not getting?" Then they build something that addresses that pain, nothing more, nothing less.

To obsess over the problem, talk to your audience. Listen to their complaints. Study their behavior. Do this first before diving in.

Discipline Turns Problems into Profits

Discipline isn't flashy or cool. It's you showing up to write one page, make one call, or test one idea, even when you're tired or uninspired. It's choosing progress over perfection.

Millionaires lean on discipline to turn problems into profits. They create systems and have daily habits, routines, and processes that keep them moving forward. They don't wait for inspiration; they work through the slog. For example, instead of dreaming about a perfect app, they'll launch a bare-bones version to test demand. If it flops, they pivot. If it works, they scale. Either way, they're learning and moving closer to the money.

Here's how to build discipline:

- **Start Small**: Commit to one tiny action daily. Write a few paragraphs a day like I do. Email one potential client. Small wins help build momentum.

- **Track Progress**: Log your actions using a simple spreadsheet or app. Seeing your streak grow keeps you accountable.

- **Cut Distractions**: Identify what pulls you off track. Turn off notifications, unplug from social media, stop overthinking, and set boundaries.

- **Focus on Inputs, Not Outcomes**: You can't control sales or virality, but you can control effort. Put in the reps, and results will come.

The Money Follows the Problem-Solver

Money comes naturally when you obsess over a problem and back it up with discipline. Look at any successful business in your locale. They started small and dreamed of providing value, high-quality service, then multiplying and scaling. Eventually, they were able to solve problems that customers had: faster delivery, sustainable transportation, high-quality products, locally sourced, and having a cozy place to work. The money followed because they delivered value consistently.

Dreams Fuel the Fire, Discipline Builds the House

Don't get me wrong, dreams matter. They're the spark that gets you moving, and the vision that keeps you motivated. But without discipline, they're just smoke.

Discipline over dreams means choosing the hard work of problem-solving over the fleeting high of a perfect idea. It means showing up when no one's watching, tweaking when no one cares, and trusting that every step forward counts.

Obsess over the problem, not the product. The money will come, and when it does, it'll be because you earned it.

THE ENGINE OF SOLUTIONS

CHAPTER 28

Avoiding Burnout

The grind is real. I've been there working late nights, chasing goals, fueled by coffee and ambition, only to wake up the next day and repeat the same thing. Burnout doesn't just sap your energy; it kills your passion, dulls your hunger, and makes even the things you love feel like chores. Somedays, you do not feel like getting out of bed. Success isn't worth much if it leaves you empty.

Millionaires and high achievers don't just work hard; they work smart, while sustaining momentum without flaming out. They stay hungry and passionate by balancing intensity with intention.

Avoiding burnout isn't about working less; it's about working better, protecting your sanity, and building a life that fuels your drive.

The Burnout Trap

Burnout sneaks up on you. It starts with small signs of irritability, trouble focusing, and dreading tasks you used to love. For many, pushing through was the answer, and resting was for the weak. Then, when butnout finally hits you at some point, you become unproductive, miserable, and even question yourself why you even got started.

Burnout isn't a badge of honor; it's a warning. It's your mind and body telling you that your pace isn't sustainable.

Millionaires know this. They don't glorify, but they prioritize longevity. They understand that success is a marathon, not a sprint, and burning out means you're out of the race. So they take it slow and steady without sweating it while making well-calculated moves.

Sustaining Momentum: Work Smarter, Not Harder

The key to avoiding burnout is sustaining momentum without sacrificing your health or passion. This means building systems that keep you moving forward without draining your soul. Here's how to sustain momentum:

- **Prioritize High-Impact Tasks**: Focus on the 20% of actions that drive 80% of your results. Identify your high-impact tasks and protect time for them.

- **Batch Your Work**: Group similar tasks together to minimize mental switching. Batching saves energy and keeps your work flowing.

- **Set Boundaries**: Millionaires don't let work bleed into every hour of the day. They may stop working at 6.00 pm, and then it's family time. Boundaries protect your energy and time. It will also keep you hungry for tomorrow's start.

- **Automate and Delegate**: Use tools to handle repetitive tasks such as using scheduling software, accounting apps, and virtual assistants.

Staying Hungry: Feeding Your "Why"

Why are you doing what you are doing? Passion fades when you lose sight of why you're doing this. We get so caught up in hitting revenue goals that we forget why we started our business in the first place. Reconnecting with your "why" keeps you hungry, even when the grind feels heavy. Always know your "why" and know why you are doing it.

Do you have an answer to why you go to work every day, and why you are making money by trading time, and what for and for whom?

If you do not have the answer to all of these questions, it's time to know your "Why" and get answers from within you.

To stay passionate:

- **Revisit Your Purpose**: Write down why you started. Is it freedom? Impact? Security? Keep that note where you can see it daily. Stick it in front of you on your vision board.

- **Celebrate Progress**: Big wins are rare, but small wins are constant. Did you land a client? Finish a project? Celebrate those. I keep a "win jar" where I drop notes about daily achievements. On tough days, they remind and compel me to focus on my goals.

- **Mix It Up**: Monotony kills passion. Try new approaches in your line of work. Find ways to keep your work fresh and reignite your excitement each day.

Protecting Your Energy: The Non-Negotiables

Your energy is your most valuable asset. Millionaires treat it like gold, guarding it with non-negotiable habits. When burnout sets in, connect to your basics and listen to what your mom taught you. Here's how to protect your energy:

- **Sleep Like a Pro**: Seven to eight hours of sleep isn't a luxury; it's a necessity. It helps maximize your energy, clarity, and creativity.

- **Move Your Body**: Exercise isn't just for your body. It's for your mind too. A 20-minute walk or gym

261

session can reset your mood. It's like hitting a mental refresh button.

- **Connect with Others**: Isolation fuels burnout. Spend time with people who uplift and inspire you.

- **Unplug Regularly**: Take time away from screens and headphones. Unplug, unsubscribe, and unwind from all that external noise, and it's amazing to know how much clearer we think after that break. Moreover, how do we know if the radio waves, sound waves, microwaves, WiFi, Bluetooth, etc., to which we are regularly exposed are safe to our bodies and health? No one seems to question it, and everyone seems to go about their lives unhindered.

Passion as a Renewable Resource

Passion isn't finite, it's renewable, but only if you nurture it. Millionaires don't run on fumes; they build lives that recharge their drive. When I started treating my energy and passion as priorities, not afterthoughts, I stopped dreading work and started loving it again.

Avoiding burnout doesn't mean slowing down; it means working with intention. It's about building systems to sustain momentum, staying connected to your purpose, and protecting your energy like it's your most valuable investment. Because it is. Stay hungry, stay passionate, and keep going, not by grinding yourself into dust, but by building a life that lights and fuels your inner fire.

CHAPTER 29

Building Wealth That Lasts

Wealth isn't just about having money today; it's about having it tomorrow, the next year, and for future generations. Most of us learn this lesson the hard way when we blow through a $10,000 vacation in a week. In addition to this, we purchase a few shiny gadgets, fancy souvenirs, and expensive gifts. Everything feels great until our bank balance hits ZERO.

Our mindset is that we are thinking for today, not tomorrow or the next five years. We think in days, not decades, and it will cost us big time. Most people make the same mistake by chasing short-term highs instead of building wealth that endures, which takes decades. It's much easier to spend on credit than it is to save paper money and spend it.

When you use cash, you will feel the pain and the bite of losing it when you see it leave your hands. But, when using plastic and living on credit, you do not feel anything while spending, but it will sink you when you see your credit card statement. Then what? You panic and sweat, then freeze.

Millionaires don't just build wealth; they build *lasting* wealth. They think that in decades, not days, they will make choices that compound over time to create financial security and legacy. This isn't about hoarding money or living like a miser, but it's about creating systems, making smart investments, and aligning your actions with your long-term goals. Here's how to shift your mindset and build wealth that stands the test of time.

The Mindset Shift: Decades Over Days

I thought wealth was about big paychecks and flashy purchases when I was younger.

I'd see someone with a new car or a designer watch and think, "That's success." It was a perception that was society-driven, which has been drilled into our minds since an early age. But in reality, millionaires teach me that real wealth isn't what you show off with material possessions, but what you keep. The less you spend, the more you will have. It's the money that works for you, grows quietly, and gives you freedom years down the line.

Stealth wealth has become the new norm for the wealthy. You may never know who is a billionaire or poor these days. Your neighbor with that brand new luxury car may be broke, and the old farmer in your neighboring town who is dressed shabbily and lives in a 1200 square foot home is a billionaire. Again, you will never know.

Thinking in decades means asking, "Will this decision make me richer in 10 years, or just today?" It's choosing a rental property over a luxury vacation, investing in skills over splurging on trends, or saving 20% of your income instead of spending it all on luxury items. You have a choice to make here.

This mindset shift isn't about sacrifice, it's about prioritizing your future self. Every dollar you save, invest, or earn today is a seed planted for creating a forest of wealth 10 years from now. *The question is: Are you prepared for delayed gratification, and what does your mind have to say about it?*

Building Systems for Wealth Creation

Lasting wealth doesn't come from one-off wins; it comes from systems that generate value year after year. Millionaires don't rely on willpower; they build systems like clockwork.

Here's how to create wealth-building systems:

- **Automate Investments**: Set up automatic transfers to investment accounts before you can spend any of your income. Start small and grow big.

- **Diversify Income Streams**: Don't rely on one source of income, namely a paycheck. If you have only one income source, that income stream dries up. Now what? Create many more revenue-generating channels.

- **Track and Optimize**: Review your finances monthly. You may use a simple spreadsheet to monitor income, expenses, and investments. It may help spot leaks and prevent unnecessary expenditures.

- **Reinvest Profits**: Instead of pocketing every dollar, reinvest in your business, skills, and assets.

These systems aren't glamorous, but they're the backbone of wealth that lasts. They ensure your money grows even when you're not working.

Invest in Assets That Grow and Appreciate

Millionaires don't just hoard money; they invest in assets that appreciate over time. They do not put their money in a savings account in a bank earning 0.001%. When factoring in inflation, your money in the bank may lose value yearly. Wealth that lasts comes from owning things that tend to appreciate over time: stocks, real estate, businesses, and your skills.

Here's how to invest for the long haul:

- **Stock Market**: Historically, it has performed well. But with the ups and downs, you may participate if you have the stomach to weather the storm. There are no guarantees, and the spread gets taxed on realization of the gains.

- **Real Estate**: Properties may potentially generate passive income and may appreciate. It may also be a hedge against inflation. Requires upfront capital and constant management and maintenance.

- **Investing in Yourself**: Investing in skills and education often gives the highest return. This may depend on the field and the demand. You can learn anything these days on the internet. Maximize its use. There is no excuse to be financially illiterate these days. Watch videos, listen to podcasts, and read books.

- **Businesses**: Start or invest in business ventures that solve real problems. You may even want to consider an existing cash flow-ready business that may come at a premium.

The key is to focus on assets that compound, things that grow faster the longer you hold them. Avoid liabilities like expensive cars or depreciating gadgets that drain your wealth.

Protect Your Wealth

Building wealth is only half the battle; protecting it is just as crucial. Millionaires don't just chase returns; they shield their wealth from risks and predators.

Here's how to protect what you build:

- **Start with one, then diversify**: Don't put all your eggs in one basket. Spread investments across stocks, real estate, and other assets to reduce and mitigate risk.

- **Insurance**: Life, health, and property insurance are non-negotiable. They're not something we may like, but they are "supposedly" a safety net that may offer some degree of protection. You will need to read the fine print. What you are promised is not what you may receive when you need it the most.

- **Emergency Fund**: Keep 3-6 months of expenses in a liquid account. It may provide a buffer against unexpected events and setbacks.

- **Due Diligence**: Research every investment. Learn it. Understand it. Never invest in something you do not know or understand. Know your numbers well.

Legacy: Wealth Beyond Your Lifetime

Wealth that lasts isn't just for you; it's for your family, community, and causes you care about. Thinking in decades means planning for a legacy. It's not about being a millionaire or a billionaire; it's about leaving something behind that matters.

Consider:

- **Estate Planning**: A simple will or trust ensures your wealth goes where you want. It may give you peace of mind knowing all affairs are in order.

- **Teaching Wealth Principles**: Share what you know with people you meet who are curious to learn. Pick a niche, write a book, and share your knowledge.

- **Giving Back**: Allocate a portion of your wealth to causes you believe in. Even $100 a month to a charity can create a ripple effect. It may also help someone somewhere whom you may never meet in your life. That's a noble deed, indeed.

The Long Game Wins

Building wealth that lasts isn't about quick wins or getting rich quickly. It's about thinking in decades, and not in days. It's setting up systems that compound, investing in assets that grow, protecting what you build, and planning for a legacy transfer.

Wealth that lasts gives you the freedom, security, safety, and stability, as well as the financial means to help anyone you want. You can also make a global impact. It's not about how much you make today, but how much you keep tomorrow. Start planting those seeds now, and in a decade, you'll be amazed to see the forest you'll have created.

PART 7

TRANSITIONING FROM BEING RICH TO BECOMING ULTRA–WEALTHY
Design a Life Filled with Abundance

CHAPTER 30

Escape the Time-for-Money Trap

Nothing is wrong with a job or working a 9-5 job by trading time for money, but incomes have not kept up with inflation. How does one support themselves and their families? To make matters worse, wages have stagnated, the cost of living has been going up steadily, and savings have gone way down; the number of people living on credit has been steadily increasing, and living on debt has become the new norm. Stress has increased, family life seems irrelevant; Sickness has skyrocketed, and preventive medicine does not seem to exist. Financial literacy is never taught in schools, and kids and adults live in the darkness of Financial Ignorance. People work 2 to 3 jobs daily, often sacrificing sleep, health, and family life. Never in the history of Man have we seen this happen.

Where are we going and what direction are we taking? Are we heading in the wrong direction?

Now, let's talk about you. You've hustled hard. You've earned your place, proven your worth, and built something real. Back then, when you were starting out, the grind was necessary, those late nights, the sacrifices, the relentless push to make ends meet. But let's be honest: you didn't come this far to stay chained to the clock.

You didn't pour your heart into your work just to trade hours for dollars, trapped in a cycle that feels like progress but smells like pressure. The truth hits like a whisper: if your income stops when you do, you're not running a business, you're running a job in disguise.

The time-for-money trap is a subtle thief. It sneaks into the lives of dentists, coaches, doctors, lawyers, consultants, and small business owners, masquerading as success. You work, you earn. You pause, and the money pauses too. You have a job, J-O-B.

Clients depend on *you*, not a system, and every break, whether for rest, travel, or life's unexpected curveballs, means a dip in your revenue. That's not freedom. *That's a leash tied to money.*

The Time-for-Money Trap: What It Is and Why It Hurts?

The time-for-money trap is a cycle where your income is tethered to the hours you put in. Whether you're a salaried employee clocking in at 9 am or an executive juggling client calls at 8 pm, the equation is the same: no work, no pay. This may apply to doctors too. It's a model that may limit your potential because there are only so many hours a day. You can't scale time, so you can't scale your income either.

What is your hour worth? How much can you charge for it based on your profession and experience? What is your number? Most people have no idea what their hour is worth. Say it's $250 an hour. Sounds decent, right? But what happens when you're sick, vacationing, or want to take a week off to see your family? The money stops. Or maybe you're a consultant who's booked solid, but your calendar is so packed you're turning away clients. You're at capacity but still not hitting your financial goals and monthly numbers. The trap tightens. There are constraints here that are keeping you stuck.

The consequences go beyond money. The constant pressure to work more, hustle harder, and squeeze in one more project erodes your well-being. Burnout creeps in. Stress festers. You're so busy chasing the next paycheck that you lose sight of why you started this in the first place, your dreams, your passions, and the life you wanted to build.

The time-for-money trap may not just cap your income; it may cap your freedom, growth, and joy. But literally 99% of us are doing it without ever questioning it. Not because we want to, but because we have to. That's probably 6.9 billion people on this Planet who will be clocking in daily for the next 60 years.

Are you caught in its grip? Here's the Gut Check

Take a moment to reflect. You might be in a trap if:

- You dread taking time off because it means no income.

- Your earnings reset to zero every month, no matter how hard you worked before.

- You only get paid when you're actively working

- You're the bottleneck: clients wait on *you*

- A single disruption - sickness, travel, or even a holiday- can cut your revenue.

If any of this feels familiar, you're not alone. But you don't have to stay stuck. The path to freedom starts with seeing the trap for what it is and choosing to build something better.

In addition to your primary job, you should have a side hustle that could help bring in some extra revenue. Over time, create multiple streams of income to help take control of your finances and your life.

The Cost of Staying Trapped

Staying in the time-for-money trap comes with a steep price. First, there's the obvious: your earning potential is capped. No matter your skill level, you can't work 100 hours a week to double your income. The math doesn't scale. If you're a coach charging per session, you must work with dozens of clients monthly to hit your financial goals. That's not a business, it's a treadmill.

Then there's the loss of control. When your income depends on your time and what you put in, you may be at the mercy of others' schedules and what they dictate. Then there is office politics. Clients and your boss at work will get to dictate when you need to work. Deadlines may dictate how you live. Want to take a spontaneous trip or spend a day with your kids? Tough luck-your calendar may say no. This lack of flexibility isn't just inconvenient; it becomes a cage.

Worse still, the trap stifles your growth. When you're consumed with trading hours for money, you don't have the space to dream bigger. You're too busy putting out fires to innovate, too tired to learn new skills, too stretched to chase the ideas that once lit you up. Over time, this can leave you feeling unfulfilled, disconnected from your purpose, and stuck in a life smaller than you deserve and hoped for. And this becomes monotonous.

The Promise of Freedom

Escaping the time-for-money trap isn't just about making more money; it's about reclaiming your life. *When your income isn't tied to your hours, you unlock a world of possibilities:*

- **Unlimited Earning Potential**: By building systems and income streams that don't rely on your time, you can earn more without working more.

- **Control Over Your Life**: Imagine setting your schedule, saying yes to what matters, and no to what doesn't without worrying about your bank account.

- **Pursuing Your Passions**: With time freed up, you can focus on the work that excites you, whether creating, exploring, or simply living more fully. You may also delegate low-value tasks to focus on high-value ones.

- **Better Balance**: Less time chasing paychecks means more time for self-care, relationships, and the moments that make life rich.

- **Long-Term Wealth**: Passive income and smart investments help build a foundation for financial security, so you're not just surviving—you're thriving.

This isn't a dream. It's a shift in how you work, think, and build. The journey starts with small, intentional steps to untether your income from your time.

Wanting to Break Free

Escaping the time-for-money trap is a process, not an overnight fix. It requires clarity, strategy, and action. *It may take a year or even a decade to transition while working your current job. You must cover all your bases and finances well before making any move. If not, you will not be on a stable foundation.*

Here's how you may want to start:

1. Assess Your Current Reality

Take a hard look at your finances. How much are you earning? How many hours are you working to earn it? What are your expenses, and where can you optimize? Calculate how much you need to live the life you want and not just to get by. This number is your Guiding Star and your focus. How much is your HOURLY NUMBER? It's not about greed; it's about creating space for freedom.

2. Shift Your Pricing Mindset

Stop charging for your time. You're not a laborer, you're a professional with expertise. Your price may be based on the *value* you plan to deliver, not the hours you spend working on the project. If you're a fitness coach and your program helps a client achieve a significant transformation, don't charge for a set number of sessions. Charge for the outcome. Audit your rates: how many clients do you need at your current prices to hit your goals? If the number feels exhausting, raise your rates and deliver exceptional value to match. Deliver the best and charge a premium for it. This may depend on various factors, too.

3. Stop the Free Work Leak

You're giving away more than you think. Those "quick" messaging app tips, uncommitted clients, or calls that stretch too long may be draining your profits. Set boundaries. Turn casual access into paid services. For example, offer a monthly retainer for ongoing advice and support. Clients value what they pay for, and you'll value the steady income. When something is free, people may not value it.

4. Explore Alternative Income Streams

Diversifying your income is key to breaking free. Look for ways to leverage your skills without trading hours:

- **Productize Your Expertise**: Turn your knowledge into digital products like eBooks, online courses, or templates. Create them once, sell them forever.

- **Build Subscriptions**: Offer a premium newsletter, content toolkits, or build a membership community with exclusive insights and access.

- **Tap Into Affiliate Income**: Recommend tools or services you love and earn commissions when others sign up.

- **License Your Work**: Let others use your frameworks, templates, or processes for a fee, creating income without extra effort.

5. Embrace Passive Income

Passive income isn't "no work," "work once, earn often." Invest in assets that generate revenue over time:

- **Real Estate**: Rental properties and other platforms can provide steady cash flow with minimal upkeep.

- **Digital Products**: Courses, eBooks, or software can scale without your constant input.

- **Investments**: Dividend-paying stocks may help grow your wealth while you focus elsewhere.

- **Digital Real Estate**: Buy digital assets that may help earn revenue through ads or products.

6. Leverage Technology and Automation

Technology is your ally. Automate repetitive tasks like social media posts and email campaigns to free up time. You may also use tools like project management software, virtual assistants, or AI-driven systems to streamline your workflow and make your life easier.

7. Master Your Time

Effective time management is your superpower. Use the 80/20 rule to focus on high-impact tasks. Block time for deep work, admin tasks, and personal growth. And don't forget self-care because burnout is the enemy of progress.

8. Rewire Your Mindset

The biggest barrier to freedom is often your own beliefs. Challenge the idea that you need to work harder to earn more. Which may be the norm, the norm we have been conditioned with. Create your norm.

Embrace a growth mindset: your skills, income, and opportunities can expand with effort and learning. Surround yourself with people who've escaped the trap. You may join communities, attend workshops, or find mentors who may inspire you. Practice mindfulness to stay grounded and focus on your bigger vision.

Pointers to help build additional income streams

- **Refine your side job:** Make sure it's aligned with your strengths and interests. A side hustle you're passionate about is more likely to thrive.
- **Schedule intentionally:** Block out time in the evenings but avoid burnout. Even short, focused sessions may lead to steady progress.
- **Track your earnings and growth:** Create a simple dashboard to monitor income from each source, so you know what's working.

Stack your income streams:

- **Active income:** Primary job, Freelancing, tutoring, consulting, or gig work.
- **Passive income**: Digital products, affiliate marketing, rental properties.

- **Hybrid income:** Online courses, subscriptions, or monetized content that requires upfront effort and pays long-term.

Breaking free from the time-for-money trap is a journey that demands action, not just aspiration. You should never let go of your primary job until you have two additional income streams that are predictable, steady, and sustainable. You've seen the trap for what it is and glimpsed the freedom that lies beyond it. Now, it's time to roll up your sleeves and build the systems that can carry you there. It may take a while, and these aren't quick fixes-they're deliberate, strategic moves to help reshape your financial future.

1: Productize Your Expertise

Your knowledge is your greatest asset. You've spent years honing your skills, solving problems, and mastering your craft. Now, it's time to package that expertise into products that can be sold repeatedly without your constant involvement. This is the essence of scalability—create once, sell forever.

- **Create Digital Products**: Turn your expertise into an online course, eBook, or template.

- **Repurpose Existing Work**: Look back at the advice you've given clients or the processes you've built. Can you turn your client onboarding checklist into a downloadable toolkit? Can your most popular workshop be transformed into a pre-recorded webinar? Repurposing helps save time and maximizes value.

- **Start Small, Scale Fast**: You don't need a 50-hour course to start. Record a 90-minute training session or write a 20-page eBook. Price it affordably to test the market, then refine based on feedback. The goal is to create something that generates income.

2: Build Recurring Revenue Streams

Consistency is the backbone of financial freedom. Instead of chasing one-off payments, create subscription or membership models that deliver ongoing value and predictable income. This shifts you from hustling to wealth-building.

- **Launch a Membership Program**: Offer exclusive content, community access, or ongoing support for a monthly fee. A business consultant might offer a premium newsletter with industry insights and templates.

- **Bundle Services into Retainers**: If you provide one-on-one services, convert ad-hoc work into retainers. Instead of charging for a single strategy session, offer a monthly package that includes check-ins, email support, and resource updates. Clients get consistent value; you get steady cash flow.

- **Leverage Content**: If you're a content creator, consider a paid newsletter where subscribers pay for exclusive insights, tutorials, or resources.

3: Monetize Your Influence

You're already recommending tools, services, and products to your network. So, why not get paid for it? Affiliate marketing and referral programs let you earn commissions without investing extra time. It's a low-effort way to generate passive income.

- **Choose Relevant Products**: Promote tools you genuinely use and trust.

- **Integrate Seamlessly**: Share your affiliate links in blog posts, newsletters, or social media content.

- **Track and Optimize**: Use analytics to see which links perform best. Focus on promoting high-converting products with generous commissions.

4: License Your Intellectual Property

Your methods, frameworks, and processes are valuable intellectual property (IP). Licensing them allows others to use your work while you earn passively. This is especially powerful for coaches, consultants, or creatives with established systems.

- **License Your Process**: If you're a business coach with a proven client acquisition system, license it to other coaches for a fee.

- **Sell Templates or Designs**: Graphic designers can license their templates to agencies or small businesses.

- **Create White-Label Products**: Develop a product that others can rebrand and sell under their brand name for a licensing fee.

5: Invest in Passive Assets

True wealth comes from ownership, not labor. Investing in assets that generate income over time is a long-term strategy to escape the time-for-money trap. While this often requires upfront capital, the returns can be life-changing.

- **Real Estate**: You may purchase a rental property and rent it out. You may outsource the management aspect of it for a fee.

- **Stock Market**: Investing and reinvesting the dividends may help compound your returns over time, creating a growing income stream.

- **Digital Real Estate**: Certain platforms let you purchase sites with proven revenue.

- **Royalty-Based Income**: If you're creative, explore royalty opportunities like publishing a book, licensing music, or creating stock photography.

6: Automate and Delegate

Technology is your escape hatch. Automating repetitive tasks and delegating low-value work allows you to focus on high-impact activities like strategy, creation, or relationship-building.

- **Automate Processes**: Use tools to connect apps and automate workflows

- **Outsource Tasks**: Hire a virtual assistant for administrative work like scheduling or invoicing.

- **Use AI Tools**: You may leverage AI for content creation, customer service chatbots, or data analysis.

7: Protect Your Time

Your time is your most precious resource. Guard it fiercely and optimize it ruthlessly. Effective time management isn't about doing more; it's about doing what matters.

- **Apply the 80/20 Rule**: Identify the 20% of tasks that drive 80% of your results.

- **Use Time-Blocking**: Reserve specific hours for deep work. Stick to the schedule.

- **Say No**: Decline low-value projects and clients that don't align with your goals. Every "yes" to the wrong thing is a "no" to your freedom.

- **Invest in Self-Care**: Take time to take care of your health.

8: Cultivate a Freedom Mindset

Your mindset is the foundation of your escape. You'll stay stuck if you believe you're destined to trade time for money forever. You'll find a way forward if you believe in abundance and possibility.

- **Challenge Limiting Beliefs**: Challenge yourself, do what you want, and follow your goals. Because no one else will.

- **Surround Yourself with Winners**: Join like-minded communities of entrepreneurs who've escaped the trap.

- **Practice Gratitude and Abundance**: Reflect daily on what's working—your skills, your progress, your opportunities. A scarcity mindset will keep you trapped; an abundance mindset can help open doors.

- **Stay Curious**: Commit to learning. Read books and listen to podcasts on passive income. Knowledge fuels confidence. Keep learning and be a lifelong learner.

THE ARCHITECTURE OF SERVICE

CHAPTER 31

The Freedom Formula

You're standing at a crossroads. On one side, there's the familiar grind, the endless to-do lists, the late nights, the nagging feeling that you're running all over the place. On the other hand, there's a path less traveled: a life where your business hums along, generating wealth while you sip coffee with a friend, travel to a new Country, or sit still, knowing your future is secure. This isn't a fantasy, it's the promise of the Freedom Formula.

The Freedom Formula isn't a quick fix or a get-rich scheme. It's a deliberate strategy to untether your income from your hours, your success from your sweat, and your dreams from your doubts. It's about leveraging three powerful forces: time, teams, and technology, to build a business that doesn't just survive but thrives without you.

Picture yourself a year from now. Your inbox isn't maxed out. Your team handles the day-to-day with confidence. Your systems churn out results like a well-oiled machine. You're not just working, and you're creating, leading, and living. This chapter is your blueprint to make that vision real.

Let's break it down.

Why the Freedom Formula Matters?

You didn't start your business to become its employee. Yet here you are, juggling tasks, chasing deadlines, and wondering if this is what success feels like. The truth? Success isn't measured by how busy you are; it's measured by how free you are to live on your terms.

The Freedom Formula may be your escape from the hamster wheel. It's about working smarter, not harder, by harnessing:

- **Time**: Protect it, optimize it, and make it your ally, not your master.

- **Teams**: Build a group of capable people who amplify your vision, not just follow orders.

- **Technology**: Use tools to automate the repetitive, streamline the complex, and scale the impossible.

Time, Team, and Technology: This formula isn't just for tech moguls or corporate giants. It's for you, the small business owner who's ready to stop trading hours for dollars and start building a legacy. Let's dive into how to make it happen.

1: Master Your Time

Your time is your most finite resource. Every hour spent on low-value tasks is an hour stolen from your dreams. The Freedom Formula begins with reclaiming your time, not by working faster, but by working strategically.

Audit Your Hours

Start by tracking how you spend your week. Use a simple spreadsheet to log every task, emails, client calls, social media posts, invoicing, etc. Be ruthless in your honesty. You'll likely find that 80% of your results come from 20% of your efforts. The rest? It's noise.

Ask yourself:

- Which tasks could someone else do just as well, if not better?

- Which activities of mine directly drive revenue and growth?

- Where am I wasting time due to indecision?

Free up your time for what only you can do: strategizing, creating, leading.

Time-Block Like a Pro

Once you've identified high-impact tasks, protect them with **time-blocking**. Reserve specific hours for deep work, say, creating a new product or planning your next partnership. Block other hours for admin, team check-ins, and personal growth. And yes, block time for rest, too. Burnout; it's a barrier to freedom. Prevent it.

- **Morning Deep Work (9–11 AM)**: Focus on high-value tasks like product creation or strategy. No emails, no distractions.

- **Midday Admin (1–2 PM)**: Handle emails, invoicing, and quick reviews.

- **Afternoon Growth (3–4 PM)**: Learn a new skill, attend business meetings, network, or explore partnerships.

- **Evening Recharge**: Step away. Exercise, read, or spend time with loved ones.

Say No to Save your Yes

Every "yes" to a low-value task is a "no" to your bigger goals. Practice saying no to clients who don't align with your vision, to projects that drain your energy, and to meetings with no clear outcome.

By guarding your time, you get to create space for what moves the needle, whether building a partnership or simply thinking creatively.

2: Build a Team That Scales

No one can build an empire alone. The Freedom Formula hinges on surrounding yourself with people who amplify your strengths and fill in your gaps. A team isn't just hired help; it's a force multiplier that lets you focus on vision while they execute the details.

Hire for Outcomes, Not Tasks

Stop hiring people to "do stuff." Hire them to achieve results. This shift changes everything—it attracts ambitious talent and frees you from micromanaging.

For example:

- A virtual assistant (VA) isn't just for scheduling. They can manage client onboarding and help with other tasks as well, freeing you to focus on operations.

- A content creator and graphic designer may be the face of your organization. They can build a content strategy that can help drive leads.

Empower, Don't Control

Great teams thrive on trust, not oversight. Train your team thoroughly on SOPs (Standard Operating Procedures). Check in with them weekly. Let them solve problems and bring about solutions.

Start Small, Scale Smart

You don't need a 10-person team to start. Begin with one part-time VA or contractor for your most time-consuming task. As revenue grows, add specialists such as a marketer, a bookkeeper, a customer support lead, etc. Each hire should help buy back your time and boost your capacity to scale.

3: Harness Technology as Your Engine

Technology is the backbone of the Freedom Formula. It's not about chasing shiny new tools; it's about using the right ones to automate, streamline, and scale your business. The goal? Make your business run like a machine, even when you're offline.

Automate the Repetitive

Identify tasks you do repeatedly and automate them for tasks such as Client Onboarding, Social media management, and invoicing.

Streamline with Systems

Technology isn't just for automation, it's for creating seamless workflows. Use project management tools to keep tasks, deadlines, and team communication in one place.

Scale with Smart Tools

Technology lets you reach more people with less effort.

Consider:

- **Email Marketing**: Use Platforms that let you nurture thousands of leads with personalized sequences.

- **E-Commerce**: Use ecommerce platforms to sell digital products 24/7 without your involvement.

- **AI Tools**: Use tools to brainstorm content ideas, analyze trends, or draft emails, cutting hours off creative work.

Common Pitfalls to Avoid

The Freedom Formula is powerful, but it's not foolproof. Watch out for these traps:

1. **Overloading on Tools**: Don't sign up for every app. Pick one tool per system before adding more.

2. **Hiring Without Clarity**: Don't hire until you've documented your processes. A team can't execute what isn't clear.

3. **Neglecting Maintenance**: Systems and teams need regular check-ins. Review your automations and team performance monthly to catch issues early.

4. **Fear of Letting Go**: Delegating feels risky, but holding on to every task is riskier. Trust your team and systems to free your mind for bigger things.

Your First Step to Freedom

You don't need to overhaul your business overnight. Start small, but start today. Pick one element of the Freedom Formula:

- **Time**: Track your hours for one week and eliminate one low-value task.

- **Team**: Hire a VA for 5 hours a week to handle your most repetitive task.

- **Technology**: Automate one process, like scheduling or invoicing,

The Mindset of Freedom

The Freedom Formula isn't just about tactics, it's about believing you deserve a life where work serves you, not owns you.

Challenge the voice that says, "I have to do it all myself" or "I can't afford to hire." Replace it with, "I'm building a machine that works for me." Surround yourself with entrepreneurs who've done it, or join a mastermind group. Their stories will remind you that freedom is possible.

Every step you take, every task delegated, every system built, and every tool implemented is the foundation of your freedom. You're not just running a business; you're designing your life.

The Freedom Formula allows you to dream bigger, work smarter, and live fuller. Time, teams, and technology are your levers. Pull them, and watch your world expand.

CHAPTER 32

Reinvest in Bigger Problems

You've tasted freedom, time to think, recreate, and breathe deep. But freedom isn't the finish line; it's the launchpad. The question now isn't "How do I survive?" but "How do I soar?" The answer lies in chasing bigger problems not just for profit, but for purpose.

When you reinvest your success into tackling larger problems, you don't just grow your business, you redefine what's possible for yourself and the world around you.

The Power of Bigger Problems

Small problems keep you busy; big problems make you essential. Solving a small problem like designing a single logo or coaching one client pays the bills, but caps your income potential. Tackling a bigger problem like streamlining branding for an entire industry or transforming how people approach personal growth creates a ripple effect. It positions you as a leader, attracts bigger opportunities, and unlocks exponential rewards.

Think of it like climbing a mountain. You've conquered the foothills: your systems are solid, your team is capable, and your income is steady. Now, the peaks loom ahead: complex, daunting, and thrilling. These are the problems that demand more of you: more creativity, more courage, more strategy. But they also deliver more: more influence, and more revenue.

Bigger problems aren't just harder; they're magnetic. They pull in better clients, sharper partners, with a deeper purpose. They force you to grow, to innovate, to become the person who can solve them. And in doing so, they help transform your business from a service into a movement.

Why Reinvest in Bigger Problems?

Reinvesting your success: time, money, and skills into larger challenges isn't about greed but growth. Here's why it matters:

- **Amplify Your Impact**: Solving a problem for one person is rewarding; solving it for thousands is transformative.

- **Attract Premium Opportunities**: Big problems draw big players. When you tackle industry-wide challenges, you attract high-value clients, partners, and investors who want to align with your vision.

- **Multiply Your Income**: Bigger problems command higher prices. A consultant solving a company's inefficiencies might charge $50,000; one solving an industry's supply chain crisis can charge $500,000 or more.

- **Stay Ahead of the Curve**: The world evolves fast. You can position yourself as a pioneer by tackling emerging problems like AI-driven customer service or sustainable business practices.

- **Fuel Your Passion**: Big problems ignite your purpose. They're the challenges that get you out of bed, not because you have to, but because you can't wait to make a dent in the universe.

How to Identify Bigger Problems?

Not every problem is worth your energy. The right ones align with your strengths, vision, and the world's needs. Here's how to find them:

1. **Look at Your Current Wins**

2. Reflect on the problems you've already solved. What patterns do emerge? Your past successes are clues to bigger opportunities.

3. **Listen to Your Audience**

4. Your clients, followers, and community are a goldmine of insights. What do they complain about? What keeps them up at night?

5. **Spot Industry Gaps**

6. Every industry has blind spots, inefficiencies, outdated practices, or unmet needs. What's broken and no one's fixing? These gaps are your entry points.

7. **Think Exponentially**

8. Instead of solving for one, solve for many. Shift from individual solutions to systemic ones.

9. **Align with Your Why**

10. The biggest problems are the ones that light you up. What frustrates you about the world? What change do you want to see? Your purpose fuels your persistence.

Strategies to Tackle Bigger Problems

Once you've identified a problem worth solving, it's time to act. Here's how to reinvest your resources strategically:

1. Reinvest Your Revenue

Your business is now an asset, not just a paycheck. Use its profits to fund bigger ventures:

- **Develop Scalable Products**: Turn your expertise into a product that solves a widespread problem. You could create an app for automated budgeting, reaching thousands instead of dozens.

- **Fund Research and Development**: Invest in prototyping solutions. A fashion designer noticing waste in fast fashion might develop a line of eco-friendly fabrics, testing small batches before scaling.

- **Market at Scale**: Use profits to amplify your reach. Run targeted ads to promote your new solution to a broader audience.

2. Leverage Your Team's Strengths

Your team isn't just for operations, they're your co-creators. Involve them in solving bigger problems:

- **Brainstorm Collectively**: Hold a quarterly "big problem" session. Ask your team: What challenges do our clients face that we could solve at scale?

- **Upskill Strategically**: Train your team in skills that align with the problem.

- **Delegate Innovation**: Assign a team member to lead a new initiative, like launching a pilot program. Empower them to own the outcome, not just the tasks.

3. Harness Technology for Scale

Technology is your megaphone. It helps you amplify your ability to solve problems at scale.

- **Build Platforms**: Create a digital hub for your solution.

- **Use Data Insights**: Analyze customer data to uncover deeper problems.

- **Automate Delivery**: Use various platforms to deliver scalable courses with minimal effort through automation without manual input.

4. Partner for Impact

Big problems often require big networks. Amplify your reach:

- **Collaborate with Influencers**: Partner with thought leaders who already address the problem.

- **Join Industry Coalitions**: Align with organizations tackling the same issue.

- **License Your Solution**: If your solution is a software, framework, or a tool, license it to others to solve the problem at scale.

5. Iterate and Scale Gradually

Big problems don't need big solutions right away. Start with a minimum viable solution (MVS):

- **Test Small**: Launch a pilot.

- **Gather Feedback**: Use surveys to refine your solution. Ask: Does this solve your problem? What's missing?

- **Scale Smart**: Once validated, expand. Partner with distributors, invest in marketing, or automate delivery to reach more people.

The Mindset of a Problem-Solver

Tackling bigger problems requires a shift in how you see yourself. You're no longer just a business owner; you're in a position to help make change.

You may embrace these beliefs:

- **Problems Are Opportunities**: Every challenge is a chance to create value. A broken system in your industry? That's your invitation to innovate.

- **Failure Is Feedback**: Big problems are complex. If your first solution flops, it's not a failure; it is a source for data. Refine and retry.

- **Abundance Over Scarcity**: There's enough impact and income. Solving bigger problems doesn't diminish others; it elevates everyone.

Surround yourself with inspiration. Join a mastermind group or attend industry conferences to spark ideas. Your mindset can help fuel your mission.

Things to Avoid

Chasing bigger problems is exhilarating, but missteps can derail you:

1. **Biting Off Too Much**: Don't tackle a global crisis on day one. Start with a niche problem you can solve well.

2. **Ignoring Your Core**: Don't abandon your existing business to chase a new idea. Reinvest gradually while maintaining your foundation.

3. **Skipping Validation**: Test your solution before going all-in. A $500 pilot is better than a $50,000 flop.

4. **Going It Alone**: Big problems need collaboration. Don't shy away from partnerships or mentors who can guide you.

Your First Step to Tackling Bigger Problems

You don't need to solve world hunger tomorrow. Start where you stand:

- **Reflect**: What's one problem your clients or industry face that you could solve at scale? Write down three ideas.

- **Research**: Research and uncover pain points.

- **Act**: Pick one idea and create a small pilot program by testing it with 10 customers and refine based on the feedback received.

Ask yourself: *What problem am I uniquely positioned to solve?* Your skills, experience, and passion are the clues.

The Legacy of Big Problems

Solving bigger problems isn't just about income; it's about making a much bigger impact. It's about building something that outlives you, changes lives, and leaves the world better than you found it. Every dollar you reinvest, every hour you redirect, every partnership you forge is a step toward a legacy that matters.

You've already proven you can survive. Now, it's time to thrive. Pick a problem bigger than you've dared to dream. Leverage your time, your team, and your technology. The world is waiting for your solution, and your future is waiting for you to build it.

COUNSEL AND KIN

CHAPTER 33

Keep It Simple, Scale Wisely

You're on the cusp of something big. Your systems are working for you, your team is growing, and you're tackling problems that matter. The temptation now is to go bigger with more features, tools, markets, and everything. But here's the truth: complexity is the silent killer of progress. The more you pile on, the more you risk losing sight of what made you successful in the first place.

Simplicity isn't a sacrifice, it's a superpower. It sharpens your focus, delights your customers, and fuels sustainable growth. Let's dive into how to strip away the clutter and scale with clarity.

Why Simplicity Wins?

Complexity feels productive. Adding new services, chasing every trend, and building intricate systems to impress is tempting. But complexity breeds confusion for you, your team, and your customers. It slows you down, inflates costs, and dilutes your impact. Simplicity, on the other hand, amplifies value. It makes your business easier to run, your offerings easier to understand, and your growth easier to sustain.

Think of the brands you admire. A fitness app with a clean, intuitive interface. A consultant who solves one core problem better than anyone else. They don't try to be everything; they master what matters. That's the secret: do less, but do it extraordinarily well and stay in your lane.

When you keep it simple, you:

- **Save Time**: Fewer moving parts mean less to manage, fix, or explain.

- **Boost Clarity**: Customers choose you because they understand your value instantly.

- **Scale Effortlessly**: Simple systems are easier to replicate, automate, and expand.

- **Stay Focused**: You pour energy into what drives results, not distractions.

Simplicity isn't about cutting corners; it's about cutting out what doesn't count. Scaling wisely means growing your impact without multiplying your headaches.

The Trap of Overcomplication

As you scale, complexity creeps in like uninvited guests. You add new tools to "optimize" workflows, only to spend hours learning them. You expand your offerings to attract more customers, only to confuse your core audience. You hire more people to handle growth, only to get bogged down in micromanagement.

The lesson? More isn't always better. Scaling wisely means saying no to what doesn't align and yes to what amplifies your core value.

How to Keep It Simple?

Simplicity is a discipline. It requires ruthless prioritization and a commitment to value over vanity. Here's how you could embed it in your business:

1. Define Your Core Value

What's the one thing your business does better than anyone else? Everything, including your products, processes, and marketing, should orbit around it.

- **Ask**: What problem do my customers thank me for solving? What's the simplest way to deliver that solution?

2. Streamline Your Offerings

More products don't always mean more revenue. A cluttered portfolio confuses customers and overwhelms your team. Instead, focus on high-impact offerings that deliver outsized value.

- **Audit Your Services**: List everything you offer. What generates the most revenue? Hold on to the top performers and phase out the rest.

- **Create One Signature Solution**: Package your core value into an irresistible product or service.

- **Test Before Expanding**: Want to add a new service? Pilot it with a small group first. If it doesn't outperform your core offering, scrap it.

3. Simplify Your Systems

Complex systems break under pressure. As you scale, keep your processes lean and your tech stack minimal.

- **Use the "Two-Tool Rule"**: Aim for no more than two tools for each system.

- **Document Simply**: Create SOPs that anyone can follow. Use bullet points, and not paragraphs.

- **Automate Only What Works**: Don't automate a broken process. Test it manually first, then use tools to connect apps.

Tip: Review your systems quarterly. Ask: Is this tool saving time or creating more work? If it's the latter, replace or eliminate it.

4. Communicate with Clarity

Your customers and team need to understand your vision instantly. Overcomplicated messaging or instructions can lead to confusion and lost opportunities.

- **Simplify Your Pitch**: Boil your value proposition to one clear sentence.

- **Train well**: When onboarding team members, focus on outcomes, not minutiae.

- **Be Transparent with Customers**: Avoid jargon or vague promises. A clear message such as: "30-day money-back guarantee" beats any "industry-leading satisfaction assurance."

How to Scale Wisely?

Scaling doesn't mean adding more; it means amplifying what works. Here's how to grow without losing your simplicity edge:

1. Double Down on What's Working

Identify your top-performing product, service, or channel. Instead of branching out, pour resources into making it even better. Check your analytics to see what drives sales and engagement. Focus there.

Tip: Ask your best customers why they chose you. Their answers will help guide where to invest your energy.

2. Expand Through Replication

Scaling doesn't always mean expanding to new markets or offering more products. Replicate your success in new contexts without reinventing the wheel. Focus on select geographic expansion, audience expansion, and partnerships.

3. Invest in Quality, Not Quantity

Scaling wisely means prioritizing depth over breadth. Focus on enhancing the customer experience, training your team, and upgrading tools sparingly.

4. Protect Your Bandwidth

As you scale, demands on your time and energy will multiply. Stay disciplined by delegating aggressively, cap your commitments, and block your time selectively.

The Mindset of Simplicity

Keeping it simple requires courage. It's saying no to shiny distractions, trusting that less can be more. Embrace these beliefs:

- **Value Trumps Volume**: One exceptional solution beats ten mediocre ones.

- **Clarity Is Magnetic**: Simple messaging attracts loyal customers and motivated teams.

- **Growth Doesn't Mean Chaos**: Scaling wisely means building on a lean, strong foundation.

Surround yourself with simplicity role models. Follow brands and entrepreneurs who nail minimalism with impact. Join a community mastermind group to share ideas on streamlining without sacrificing quality.

Pitfalls to Avoid

Simplicity sounds easy, but it requires discipline. Watch out for:

1. **Falling for "More"**: Resist adding features or services just because competitors are doing so. Stay true to your core values.

2. **Under-Simplifying**: Don't cut out so much that you compromise quality.

3. **Ignoring Feedback**: Simplicity doesn't mean to become static. Regularly ask customers and your team what's working and what's not.

4. **Scaling Too Fast**: Don't expand to new markets until your core systems are rock-solid.

Your First Step towards Simplicity

Start today with just one action to simplify and scale:

- **Audit**: List your services, tools, and processes. Pick one to eliminate or streamline.

- **Refine**: Rewrite your pitch in one clear sentence. Test it with a customer.

- **Scale**: Identify one high-performing offering and brainstorm one way to amplify it.

Ask yourself: *What's one thing I can simplify to help with growth?*

CHAPTER 34

Build A Legacy, Not Just Income

You've built a business that is thriving. Systems run smoothly, partnerships amplify your reach, and your income flows without chaining you to the grind. But deep down, you know this journey isn't just about dollars in the bank. It's about leaving a mark, a ripple that will outlast you, shift perspectives, and reshape lives. This is the moment to shift your gaze from building wealth to crafting a legacy.

Legacy isn't a dusty trophy or a name on a building. It's the lives you touch, the knowledge you share, and the communities you ignite. It's about teaching others to rise, fostering spaces where ideas collide, and empowering change that echoes beyond your lifetime.

The Difference Between Income and Legacy

Income buys you freedom; legacy gives you meaning. Income pays for your bills, vacations, and security today. Legacy builds for tomorrow: through the people you inspire, the systems you share, and the change you help spark.

Legacy isn't reserved for billionaires or celebrities. It's for anyone who dares to share their hard-earned wisdom, rally others around a cause, or create something that endures. It's not about being perfect, but it's about being purposeful.

Why Legacy Matters Now?

You've climbed the mountain of survival, scaled the peaks of systems and growth. Now, you're at a vantage point where you can see further and do more. Building a legacy matters because:

- **It Multiplies Your Impact**: One person can change a life. For example, a teacher can change thousands by sharing what they know.

- **It Attracts Purpose-Driven Allies**: When you focus on legacy, you draw in people who share your vision and help amplify your work.

- **It Sustains Your Motivation**: Income can waver, and purpose can endure. But a legacy-driven mission keeps you energized even when challenges arise.

- **It Creates Resilience**: A legacy rooted in community and shared knowledge outlasts market shifts or personal setbacks.

- **It's Your Gift to the Future**: Your struggles, lessons, and wins can light the path for others, making their journey easier and the world better.

How to Build a Legacy?

Legacy isn't built by accident. It's a deliberate act of teaching, connecting, and empowering. Here's how to weave it into your business and your life.

1. Teach What You've Mastered

Your expertise is a treasure chest-don't lock it away. Sharing your knowledge doesn't diminish your value; it amplifies it. Teaching positions you as a leader and helps plant seeds for change.

- **Create Accessible Content**: Turn your expertise into a course, book, or free resource.

- **Mentor Others**: Offer one-on-one guidance or be a speaker in group workshops.

- **Open-Source Your Process**: Share your frameworks and templates for free.

2. Build a Community Around Your Mission

A legacy thrives in connection. Create a space where like-minded people can gather, learn, and grow together.

- **Start a Digital Hub**: Launch a newsletter, share strategies, and collaborate.

- **Host Events**: Organize webinars, challenges, or live events.

- **Foster Engagement**: Encourage dialogue, not just followers. Ask questions, share insights, and celebrate wins.

Tip: Keep your community focused. Define its purpose and moderate to maintain quality.

3. Empower Change Through Advocacy

Legacy isn't just about your business, it's about the dent you make in the world. Use your platform to champion a cause that aligns with your values.

- **Raise Awareness**: Share stories or data to highlight an issue.

- **Partner with Causes**: Collaborate with nonprofits and other movements.

- **Lead by Example**: Live your values publicly.

4. Create Scalable Impact

Your legacy grows when your solutions reach more people without any more effort.

- **Productize Your Wisdom**: Turn your teaching into evergreen products like eBooks, courses, or apps.

- **License Your Impact**: Let others spread your message.

- **Automate Outreach**: Use tools to send nurturing emails or to deliver courses, ensuring your knowledge spreads 24/7.

Legacy is about creating a chain reaction. One person you teach might teach ten more. One community you build might spark a movement. One change you advocate for might shift an industry.

Avoiding Legacy Pitfalls

Building a legacy is noble but not easy. Sidestep these traps:

1. **Chasing Fame Over Impact**: Focus on real change, not likes or followers. A viral post feels good but fades fast. But a mentee's success lasts longer.

2. **Spreading Too Thin**: Don't try to teach or advocate for everything. Pick one cause or niche where you can go deep.

3. **Neglecting Your Core**: Ensure your business remains stable while you pursue legacy projects. Balance impact with income.

4. **Forgetting Authenticity**: Your legacy must reflect your true values. Don't advocate for a cause just because it's trendy.

Your First Step Toward Legacy Building

You don't need a massive platform to start. Begin from where you are:

- **Teach**: Share one lesson you've learned.
- **Connect**: Start a small community.
- **Advocate**: Pick one issue you care about. Write a blog post, or share a story.

Ask yourself: *What do I want to be remembered for?* Write down one idea, a lesson, a community, and a change. Then take one action toward it today.

Legacy Is Your Story

Your legacy is the story the world will tell about you. It's not about how much you earn, but how you inspire, connect, and uplift. Every lesson you share, every community you nurture, every change you champion is a thread in that story.

You've built a business that works for you. Now, build a legacy that works for the world. Teach with generosity, connect with purpose, and empower with courage. The ripples you create today will carry your name tomorrow.

CHAPTER 35

Live the Life of a Stinking Rich Problem Solver

You've traveled a remarkable path. You've shattered the chains of trading time for money, built systems that work like a dream, and forged alliances that catapult your reach. You've simplified your hustle, tackled audacious challenges, and sown the seeds of a legacy that will outlive you.

Now, as we close *Get Stinking Rich Solving Others' Problems*, this final chapter isn't about new tactics or bigger goals. It's a heartfelt letter to you, the visionary ready to live as a **Stinking Rich Problem Solver**. Its advice is to embrace a life where every problem you solve becomes a stepping stone to wealth, impact, and a freedom that feels like flying.

This isn't about stacking cash for show or chasing fleeting wins. It's about crafting a life so rich in meaning, in purpose, in joy, and that every challenge you face feels like an invitation to create something extraordinary. Here's the wisdom to carry forward, distilled from your journey, to live as the problem solver you were born to be.

Embrace Problems as Your Canvas

Don't shy away from problems. They're your raw material, and your chance to paint a masterpiece. Every frustration, every gap, every "this could be better" is a call to action. Whether it's a client struggling to grow their business or a community's cry for change, see these as opportunities to weave value into the world.

A problem isn't a burden; it's a spark. Ask yourself daily, "What can I make better today?" That question will lead you to riches far beyond money.

Solve with Heart and Simplicity

The best solutions aren't the flashiest, they're the ones that hit the mark with clarity and care. Don't overcomplicate your answers with bells and whistles.

Strip each problem to its core: What's the real pain here? Then craft a solution that is so simple that it feels like magic. A single checklist that saves a client hours and a short video that shifts their mindset are the gems that earn you wealth and gratitude. Solve not to impress, but to help transform.

Share Your Solutions Generously

Your knowledge is a gift-don't hoard it. Share it with the World because we are not going to take anything with us when we pass. Teach what you've learned, not to gain followers, but to light paths for others. Write a book, mentor a beginner, and spark a conversation in your circle.

When you share, you don't lose anything; you multiply. Your solutions reach further, your influence grows, and the world pays you back in loyalty, opportunities, and wealth. Be the guide you wish you'd had when you started, and watch your impact ripple.

Build Bridges, Not Walls

No problem is solved alone. Surround yourself with people who challenge you, inspire you, and bring new perspectives. Collaborate with those who share your inner fire, whether it's

313

a partner who amplifies your reach or a community that rallies around your vision. Empower others to carry your solutions forward. Let them teach, adapt, and spread your ideas. Your wealth grows when you uplift others, and your freedom expands when you're not the only one holding the torch.

Keep Growing, Keep Evolving

A Rich Problem Solver never stands still. Each problem you tackle sharpens your mind and opens new doors. Don't fear missteps, they're just clues to your next breakthrough.

Stay hungry to learn, whether it's a new skill, a fresh perspective, or a bold idea from someone else's journey. The world will keep throwing problems at you; keep rising to meet them. Your growth is the engine of your riches-keep it fueled.

Root Every Solution in Purpose

Wealth without meaning is empty; freedom without joy is hollow. Anchor your problem-solving gift in a purpose that sets your soul ablaze. Why are you doing this and for what purpose?

Is it to empower families, transform businesses, or heal communities? Let that "why" guide your every choice. When challenges feel heavy, your purpose will carry you. When success comes, it will keep you grounded. A life rich in purpose is the truest wealth of all.

Savor the Riches of Freedom

You've earned the right to live on your terms. Don't let new problems pull you back into the grind. Build solutions that work without you, systems that work on their own, teams that shine, and assets that grow.

Then use your freedom to savor what matters: a morning walk, a deep conversation, or a quiet moment to dream bigger. These are the riches that make your journey worthwhile. Live boldly, love fiercely, and rest deeply. Now, you've built a life that lets you do all three.

You are a Stinking Rich Problem Solver, not because of the money in your bank account, but because of the problems you've solved. Every challenge you've faced has shaped you to be stronger, wiser, and freer. Carry this forward:

- **Seek problems** with curiosity, knowing each one holds a fortune.

- **Solve them** with simplicity, and with a relentless focus on value.

- **Share them** with generosity, building bridges to make a bigger impact.

- **Live them** with purpose, letting your "why" light the way.

The world is a mosaic of problems waiting for your touch. You've already proven you can solve them. Now make it your life's work. Not for applause, not for wealth alone, but for the thrill of creating a life so rich it spills over, lifting everyone around you.

Go solve. Go create. Go live. The riches, wealth, impact, and freedom are yours to claim.

MAKE
MONEY
UNSTOPPABLE™
Personal Finance Made Simple

Follow the journey and explore my blog

https://makemoneyunstoppable.com/

Scan this QR CODE to explore more

Index

S

T

U

V

W

Glossary

A

- **Advantageous**: Beneficial or creating a favorable position, especially in a business or strategic setting.

B

- **Believers**: Loyal followers or supporters of a vision, brand, or mission, often early adopters or evangelists.

- **Boring**: Lacking engagement or interest; may describe uninspired business ideas or content.

- **Brainstorming**: A creative thinking process used to generate ideas and solve problems collaboratively.

- **Breadcrumbs**: Small clues or steps left to guide users/customers along a journey (e.g., marketing funnel or user experience).

- **Broken**: Dysfunctional or ineffective systems, processes, or beliefs that hinder progress or results.

- **Bureaucracy**: Overcomplicated administrative systems that often stifle innovation or efficiency.

- **Burnout**: Physical or emotional exhaustion caused by prolonged stress or overwork.

C

- **Cognitive flow**: A mental state of deep focus and productivity where time seems to disappear.

- **Confidence**: The belief in one's own abilities; essential for leadership, sales, and personal growth.

- **Costing**: The process of calculating or estimating the expenses associated with a product or service.

- **Currency**: Not just money, but anything of value exchanged can include time, attention, reputation, etc.

D

- **Discomfort**: A necessary condition for growth or change; often a sign you're on the edge of a breakthrough.

- **Disruption**: A sudden shift that changes industry norms, often through innovation.

- **Disruptive**: Describes ideas or technologies that challenge the status quo.

- **Disruptor**: A person or business that initiates major change by introducing disruptive solutions.

E

- **Embankment**: A metaphorical or literal structure to hold something steady, which could represent support systems or foundational work.

- **Emotion**: A key driver in decision-making, marketing, and leadership; it can't be ignored in business.

- **Empathy**: Understanding others' feelings and perspectives; essential in leadership and marketing.

- **Entrepreneur**: A person who starts and runs a business, often characterized by innovation and risk-taking.

- **Entrepreneurs**: Plural; the community of people pursuing innovative business ventures.

- **Ergonomic**: Designed for efficiency and comfort, especially in work environments or products.

- **Ethically**: Acting with integrity and principles; crucial in building trust and long-term success.

F

- **Financial literacy**: Understanding how money works, earning, saving, investing, and budgeting.

- **Financial weight**: The emotional or psychological burden of financial stress.

- **Freedom**: The ultimate goal for many, time, money, and creative freedom.

G

- **Glamour**: Surface-level appeal or image that may mask deeper truths; often discussed in marketing or influencer culture.

H

- **Hiring**: The process of recruiting and bringing new talent into a company or project.

I

- **Imagination**: The source of innovation and creative problem-solving.

- **Immersed**: Deeply involved or absorbed; often used in learning or customer experience contexts.

- **Inconvenience**: Small pain points or friction areas that erode user satisfaction.

- **Inefficiency**: Wasted time, energy, or resources that reduce productivity or profits.

- **Innovation**: The act of creating new and better solutions; core to business evolution.

- **Insurance**: Protection against risk; used both literally (financial) and metaphorically (emotional security).

- **Intellectual Property**: Legal rights to creations of the mind, like inventions, brands, and content.

- **Intentional**: Done with purpose and design; opposed to accidental or reactive.

- **Intimate**: Close and personal; important for trust in relationships, especially in coaching or branding.

L

- **Lackluster**: Dull or uninspired; usually refers to ideas, performance, or branding.

- **Legacy**: The impact or footprint you leave behind, personal or business-related.

M

- **Marginalised**: Pushed to the edge or excluded from opportunities or systems.

- **Marketing**: The art and science of promoting and selling products or services.

- **Millennials**: The generational cohort born roughly between 1981–1996; a key demographic in tech and marketing.

- **Mindset**: The set of beliefs and attitudes that shape one's actions and results.

- **Momentum**: The force that keeps actions and progress going once started.

- **Multiplier**: Something that increases value or results exponentially.

- **MVP (Minimum Viable Product)**: The simplest version of a product that can still deliver value and gather feedback.

O

- **Objections**: Reasons prospects hesitate or refuse; essential to address in sales and pitching.

- **Overprice**: Perceived to cost more than its value.

P

- **Perfecting**: The act of refining something to make it as effective or appealing as possible.

- **Physical pain**: Literal or metaphorical pain that influences behavior or decision-making.

- **Present pain**: The discomfort someone is experiencing now is often a strong motivator.

- **Pricing**: The strategy of assigning a cost to your product or service.

- **Primal**: Related to basic human instincts or needs.

- **Problem-solvers**: People or tools that resolve challenges effectively.

- **Procrastinate**: Delaying action despite knowing it has negative consequences.

- **Professional pain**: Challenges, stressors, or dissatisfaction related to work or career.

R

- **Radar**: Awareness or alertness; to be "on someone's radar" means they're paying attention.

- **Rapid**: Fast-paced; often describes change or execution.

- **Recognition**: Acknowledgement or visibility, either personal or professional.

- **Rejection**: Being turned down or dismissed; often a hurdle in sales, relationships, or entrepreneurship.

- **Relief**: The easing of a financial, emotional, or physical burden.

- **Repetition**: Consistent practice or messaging; key to mastery and marketing.

- **Reputation**: The public perception of a person or brand; often an invisible currency.

- **ROI (Return on Investment)**: The measure of benefit or profit relative to the cost.

S

- **Selling**: The act of persuading someone to buy or take action.

- **Soul-draining pain**: Deep, emotional exhaustion or disconnection from meaningful work.

- **Spiritual pain**: A sense of emptiness or misalignment with one's values or purpose.

- **Stinking Rich**: An exaggerated term for extreme wealth; often used humorously or aspirationally.

- **Surveys**: Tools for collecting feedback, opinions, or data from an audience.

T

- **Timing**: The strategic choice of when to act can make or break an opportunity.

- **Transformation**: A significant change, often for the better; a goal in personal growth and coaching.

- **Translation**: Converting one form of communication or value into another, e.g., ideas into products.

U

- **Upgrader**: A person who enhances systems, products, or processes.

- **User-generated content**: Content created by customers or community members, often used in marketing.

V

- **Validation**: External or internal confirmation that an idea, product, or belief is valuable or effective.

W

- **Wealth**: More than just money encompasses abundance, assets, freedom, and well-being.

MAKE
MONEY
UNSTOPPABLE™
Personal Finance Made Simple

Follow the journey and explore my blog

https://makemoneyunstoppable.com/

Scan this QR CODE to explore more